T0196412

IT'S ALL IN A WORD:

God, Life, and Meaning

WILLIAM E. MARSH

authorHOUSE®

AuthorHouse™
1663 Liberty Drive
Bloomington, IN 47403
www.authorhouse.com
Phone: 1-800-839-8640

© *2012 William E. Marsh. All rights reserved.*

No part of this book may be reproduced, stored in a retrieval system, or transmitted by any means without the written permission of the author.

Published by AuthorHouse 4/04/2012

ISBN: 978-1-4685-5837-1 (sc)
ISBN: 978-1-4685-5836-4 (e)

Library of Congress Control Number: 2012903976

Any people depicted in stock imagery provided by Thinkstock are models, and such images are being used for illustrative purposes only. Certain stock imagery © Thinkstock.

This book is printed on acid-free paper.

Because of the dynamic nature of the Internet, any web addresses or links contained in this book may have changed since publication and may no longer be valid. The views expressed in this work are solely those of the author and do not necessarily reflect the views of the publisher, and the publisher hereby disclaims any responsibility for them.

INTRODUCTION

Ah, to speak. From the moment people appeared on this planet, they have spoken, have talked about and described themselves and their world with speech. We have made speech the foundation of everything we think, say, and do.

But why do we speak? Though we speak for many reasons, most of all, we speak because we have purpose. We have a point. And we have a point because we live in a world which has a point, a reason to be. We do not live in an accidental world, a world of randomness and caprice, but in a world which was created, a world which was created, as it happens, by speech. We speak because we have been intentionally spoken into existence.

But how do we know this? How do we know that we have been spoken into existence? We know because long ago, at a pivotal point in space and time, the speech that created the world appeared in it. For a few years, a few remarkable years, that which created became the created. The eternal became mortal, the forever terminal. And we could see it, could see it clearly and distinctly. We could see the speech that made the world.

Because we could see the speech that made the world, we could see the meaning of the world. We could see what had given us and our world value and purpose. We could see why we are special, why we are important, and why we are not momentary whims of empty form and groundless imagination. We could see that we are deeply loved creations, deeply loved creations of deliberate agency and abiding purpose. We could understand that we have eternal meaning.

And part of having eternal meaning, we then come to realize, is learning to know our creator, learning to know the speech that made us: to know our beginning and end. Isn't this the point of existence?

That's what this book is all about. This book is a journey, a journey through speech. It is a journey in which we will see that because speech is the meaning of the world, the ultimate expression of the God who made us, speech is also the way to know God. And the speech that most enables us to know God is the Word who, many centuries ago, came from God to live among us, God with us, God for us, God always thinking about us: God as Jesus Christ.

This book wants you to know this Word, wants you to understand all that God's Word, expressed as it was in the person of Jesus, can be for you. It wants to help you find your true home.

So start reading. And listen for the Word, the voice of the meaning that has come.

*S*peak. That's right: speak. Say anything, anything at all. Now think about what you've done. Before you spoke, whether you talked about yourself, what you see, what you feel, what you think, or what you're imagining in your mind, it really didn't take form, didn't really become meaningful until you talked about it. By speaking about it, you brought it to life.

Many years ago, as J. R. Tolkien tells it in his Silmarillion, there was Ilúvatar. From Ilúvatar, the story goes, came the Ainur, coming forth as the fruits of Ilúvatar's thought, having always been resident in his mind. But how did the Ainur come to understand who they were? How did they learn about the world in which they found themselves?

They learned, the narrative continues, when Ilúvatar spoke to them. When he spoke to them, the Ainur realized that they could speak, too. They also realized that they could describe and define what was before them. Not only could their world be known, it could be known to them, in their way, in their time. Although their world didn't change physically—only Ilúvatar could do that—the Ainur could now make it, at least in their minds and imaginations, whatever they wanted it to be.

Their world was before them as it had never been before.[1]

Many other years ago, albeit years that, unlike those of the Silmarillion, are part of a definitive historical record, a verifiable interplay of space and time, God created human beings. According to the first chapter of Genesis (in the Hebrew Bible), after God brought the world and the cosmos in which it sits into existence, he went on, the text tells us, to create humanity.[2]

God created humanity, we are told, as male and female, shaping each one with specific intent, making each gendered being a necessary and essential counterpart and counterpoint to the other, and set them in the Garden of Eden to live, farm, and generally be who they are.

Here is a question. How did this first set of human beings, whom the text aptly names Adam (a word perhaps drawn from the Hebrew words for "blood" or "dust") and Eve (a

---

1   See J. R. R. Tolkien's *Silmarillion* (Boston: Houghton Mifflin, 1977), edited by Christopher Tolkien

2   Although those of us who deny the historical veracity of the Hebrew Bible are free to do so, they do so against the overwhelming weight of evidence that points otherwise, that the Hebrew Bible was composed by and in one of the world's longest living ethnic and religious communities over a period of many hundreds of years and has repeatedly withstood all archaeological and cultural arguments advanced against it. Though we may doubt the truth of its spiritual perspective, we cannot deny the confluence of the Hebrew Bible's descriptions of various historical events with the same events as they are attested to by centuries of universally accepted historical research. In addition, although the Hebrew creation story was written several centuries after some of the other creation stories that circulated in the ancient near east, a careful comparison of it with its counterparts indicates that it is decidedly unique in the way that it frames and describes God's activities, including his creation of human beings, in the originative process. For more, see James Pritchard, editor, *Ancient Near Eastern Texts Relating to the Old Testament* (Princeton: Princeton University, 1969).

word which seems to be based on the Hebrew verb, "to be"), learn about themselves and their world?[3]

They learned, Genesis tells us, because God taught them. God communicated with them, God spoke to them. In ways that the text does not make fully clear, but in ways whose effects are patently evident, God told them who they were, where they were living, and what they were and were not to do. As Ilúvatar did for the Ainur, the God of Genesis helped Adam and Eve, the first human beings, to uncover, define, and understand their world.[4]

How does a baby learn to talk? A baby learns to talk by listening to her parents talk to her. When her parents speak, the baby learns to speak in turn. So it was for Adam and Eve. When God talked to them, they came to grasp not only the fact of their speaking capacity, but the fact of their ability to use this capacity to formulate words and language that both they and God could understand.

Or what about the first humans of Babylonian mythology, the "black-headed ones" as they are called in the *Enuma Elish?* It was the "black-headed ones" whom the god Marduk, beloved son of Ea and Damkina, decreed he would fashion from the spilled blood of Tiamat, the dragon, the fearsome god of the salt waters who challenged the ancient gods of Mesopotamia for universal primacy. How did they come to identify themselves and their universe?

They came to know these things, the text observes, because Marduk told them. He had to: he created humans to be servants of the gods. As servants, humans needed to know how to please their master, which in turn meant that they

---

3   On these names, see Richard S. Hess, *Studies in the Personal Names of Genesis 1-11* (Winona Lake, Indiaana: Eisenbrauns, 2009).

4   Or as the *Rig Veda* observes, the "Lord of the World established Name-Giving, the first principle of language." See *Rig Veda,* translated by Wendy Doniger (New York: Penguin Press, 2005).

needed to know how to understand, describe, and deal with the world into which their masters (the gods) had put them. They needed to know how to explore and assess themselves and their world so that they could be effective servants to the ones who had made them. The ability to communicate was essential to them and their well being.[5]

Consider as well the thinking behind many native South American myths of origin. In every case, these myths underscore the importance of sound, sound as communication, sound as language. Sound as language, as these myths understood it, bequeaths discovery and presence, the realization and special awareness of being and beingness. When people began to employ sound, that is, to speak in distinctive and independent words, they attested to the reality of creation. Words and sound affirmed the meaningfulness of their world.[6]

To look at it in one more way, how, according to Greek

---

[5] For additional information on and context for this story, see Pritchard's work as it was cited above.

[6] Specifically, see the cosmological myths of the Shipibo and Canelos Quichua as they are described in *Icanchu's Drum,* by Lawrence E. Sullivan (New York: Macmillan, 1988). To view this linkage of sound and being from a slightly different angle, note the various "priestly" types in many African religions, who through dance and ritual, make meaningful, that is, accessible and plain, the language and thoughts of the gods. See Mbiti, John S., *African Religions and Philosophy* (New York: Anchor, 1970). In addition, consult the conclusion of Lewis R. Gordon in *An Introduction to Africana Philosophy* (Cambridge: Cambridge University, 2008) that language is what enables the various African cultures to establish their cultural distinctiveness: for them, language affirms individuality in the cosmos. For one more perspective on language, sound, and existence, consider how the words that inhabit Lakota Sioux creation stories, words like *Wakan* (the immortal all), *Inyan* (Rock), and *Maka* (Earth) bring meaning to life in the finished creation. On this, see *Lakota Belief and Ritual* by James R. Walker, edited by Raymond J. DeMallie and Elaine A. Jahner (Lincoln: University of Nebraska, 1991).

mythology did humanity come to know about fire? They came to know, the story goes, because Prometheus (whose name means "forethought"), the Titan son of Iapetus, secretly revealed it to them. Angry at Zeus for withholding fire from humankind, Prometheus lit a torch with the Sun's chariot of fire in order to ignite a fragment of charcoal. Setting the charcoal in a giant stalk of fennel, he slipped away to Earth, Zeus of course being unaware he was doing so, to offer it to human beings. Until the brazen Titan shared fire with humanity, people knew nothing about it. In communicating and sharing fire with them, Prometheus enabled humans to radically reshape their world.[7]

Or what can we say about the earliest hominids as they made tools in the Olduvai Gorge in the depths of East Africa? How did they learn about themselves? More importantly, how did they communicate and understand what they came to know?[8]

They learned, in some shape or form, with words. It was with words that Ilúvatar spoke to the Ainur, it was with words that God spoke to Adam and Eve, it was with words that Marduk spoke to the blackheaded ones, it was with words that Prometheus told humankind about fire, and it was

---

7   Unfortunately for Prometheus, Zeus eventually learned about what he had done, and commanded that the daring Titan be chained to a rock to which each day an eagle would come and chew out his liver. Prometheus being a Titan, however, the liver promptly grew back to its normal size. But the eagle returned the next day, and the next day, and the next, to excavate Prometheus' liver for all time. Happily, some years later, and we are not told how many, the mighty Heracles set him free. See, among other sources, Robert Graves, *The Greek Myths: I* (New York: Penguin, 1955).

8   The information on the work that the Leakeys did in Olduvai Gorge is voluminous. For a small sample, see the five volume set, *Olduvai Gorge,* edited by George Leakey and authored by Louis and Mary Leakey, published by Cambridge University Press in 2009.

with words, spoken or not, that the early hominids shared information with each other. In every instance, it was words that provided the key to understanding and meaning. Words or, put another way, speech, gave life, in a manner of speaking (no pun intended) to the world.[9]

Let's be a bit more specific. As Genesis tells it, some time after, and we are not told how much time after, he created him, God asked Adam to name the animals. Had Adam talked before? As we noted, he certainly did. God is a communicative being, and he would not make beings in his image unless they were communicative beings as well. But how did Adam decide to name the animals with the names he did?

He did so, it is very likely, on the basis of how he perceived them. Adam named the animals according to his perception of them and their activity in the environment which they both shared. He named them as he experienced them.[10]

How Adam formulated the actual act of language, however, is another matter. Based on the findings of most linguistic research, we can conclude that perhaps his ability was innate, that he was created hard wired with the capacity to form words and speak (as are we: we are born with the ability to speak).[11] His neurons (some might call these "mirror"

---

9   For a more poignant take on this conclusion, consider the final words of the late Tony Judt that, "I am fast losing control of words even as my relationship with the world has been reduced to them." Words, or as he put it, "talking," were "the point of adult existence" See "Intimations of Immortality" by Liesl Schillinger in *The New York Times,* August 15, 2010,

10   We think here of the Sanskrit word for grammar, *vyākaraṇa,* which means "analysis." In this view, language becomes not merely a way of symbolizing but a way of *understanding* what we symbolize. See Nicholas Ostler, *Empires of the World: A Language History of the World* (New York: Harper, 2005).

11   See Noam Chomsky's *On Language* (New York: New Press, 1998).

neurons[12]) were designed to respond to and describe what he saw. But how Adam was able to speak does not matter as much as that he in fact spoke. Adam spoke and described and assigned symbol and meaning to what he saw.

It may be well to pause here and note here how remarkable the fact of language is. As one writer put it, the greater wonder is that "there is language," that we humans can formulate words and speech, words and speech that, quite apart from any outside input (God inspired Adam to speak, but he did not give Adams the words to speak), we ourselves construct, shape, and express. We are remarkable communicative vehicles, a fact, which, we shall see, is foundational to our journey in this book.[13]

But let's get back to Adam. Adam of course already knew that he was living in a world, and he of course already knew that he lived in this world with the animals, but until he gave them names he did not fully know them or the world around him. He saw them, he likely heard them, he may have actually touched them, but until he used words to think and talk about them he did not permanently mark and identify them in his experience. Though they were certainly resident in and part of his experience, he had no way of distinguishing them as such. Without words to identify and describe them, without words to symbolize them, to Adam the animals were only physical entities in the garden, masses of matter that moved, fast and slow, through his nascent existence. Adam's ability to use words was crucial to constructing his world. It enabled him to give form and substance to what had previously been, in a very real way, physically indiscernible.

---

12   Consult V. S. Ramachandran's *The Tell-Tale Brain* (New York: W. W. Norton, 2010), for more information on these peculiar neurons.

13   For a very technical take on this perspective, read Christopher Fynsk's *Language and Relation* (Stanford: Stanford University, 1996).

So Adam did when he saw Eve. He had never seen a woman before; in fact, he had never seen another human being! Because he could speak, however, because he had begun to use words to describe and identify his world, he knew to do the same when he saw Eve. He immediately knew that he was to use words to describe this being who had been presented to him.

More importantly, somehow he knew what words to use. "This woman," he exclaimed, "is bone of my bones and flesh of my flesh." Of course, given the circumstances of this encounter and the similarities of Adam and Eve's physical characteristics, we might conclude that even if Adam could not use words to describe Eve, he and she would still have enjoyed communing and interacting with each other. Yet their mutual ability (we must assume that, like Adam, Eve was created with the ability to speak) to speak and verbalize their feelings made their union so much the sweeter. Subsequently, as they got to know one another, Adam and Eve began to define and describe and inscribe their world together. From this exchange came an even richer mix of definitions and understandings of experience as they, being two different people, naturally perceived the world differently. Words became even more complex, as did the world these words were used to create. Together, Adam and Eve constructed a world very different than any that either would have constructed on his or her own.[14]

But they did so with words, words with which they built their picture of reality, the world as they perceived it. They spoke their world into existence.

Of course, we understand that Adam and Eve's words

---

14   Or as quantum physics might say, in a distant echo of the philosopher Spinoza (more on him later), through observation, we create our reality, our world.

did not actually alter or shape the physical composition of their reality; what their words did do was to shape and define how they perceived it. Also, it is well to note that the text seems to indicate that Adam expressed excitement and joy when he saw Eve: as we shall see shortly, words are inherently emotional constructs. But we are not as concerned to discuss the emotional freight of Adam's words as we are concerned to see that they conveyed definition and meaning, which clearly they did. Adam's words described his affective reaction to seeing Eve. His speech captured and expressed his world.

In addition, as we observed in our mention of the early hominids of Olduvai Gorge, we communicate in many ways besides actual words, at least as we understand them today. But we definitely use words to understand what we say. We think with words, we reason with words, we communicate with words. Even if they are only rolling about in our minds, imagined, unspoken, or otherwise, words define our world.

But, you might say, what about an animal such as a cat? Does not a cat think? Does not a cat reason? Clearly, cats, along with many other animals, think and, in their own way, reason. Animals see images as much as you and I do. But as far as we know, animals do not do reason with words, at least in the sense that we know and use them. Sure, they delineate and distinguish things, and sure, they differentiate and interpret various retinal images, but that's all they do. They do not necessarily *think* with words about what they see. They do not use words to describe their experience; they simply process the images it presents to them and, in some instinctive and still not fully understood, at least to us, way, respond.

Before we go on, let's insert a caveat. Clearly, we can only use words to define and describe physical experiences because we have agreed on a common vocabulary for doing so. Words are only as useful as a given group of people consider them to be so. But this is another debate.[15]

More to the point, however, how we speak determines what we see, just as how we see determines what we say. For instance, suppose a person, for the first time, sees a car. If this person does not have a word for car in her vocabulary, she will not name it in the same way as a person who was familiar with cars will. When the Native Americans saw a train for the first time, many called it something like "great noise coming" or "rolling fire." This reflected the content of their cultural assumptions: they had no vocabulary for mechanical devices that burned rocks and shot plumes of smoke into the air. They described the train on the basis of what they knew, their cultural assumptions and the words they had been using to describe the diverse phenomena of their world. A person who sees a car for the first time will come to identify it in the same way: she will identify it on the basis of what she knows, on the basis of the informational and cultural assumptions in her brain. Most of us know that a car is a car because we have been told that it is. Those who have no categories for a car, however, do not have this luxury. They must respond to the car with the vocabulary and comprehension structures at their immediate disposal, the linguistic givens of their experience.

Again, the words we know define our world and how we see the world. Although the world remains the same regardless of how we describe it, our words create our basis for experiencing it. Our words determine how we see our world.[16]

---

15   On this, see, among others, Jacques Derrida, *Writing and Difference* (Chicago: University of Chicago, 1978).

16   For a slightly different take on this notion, consider the words of the photographer Ansel Adams, who remarked that the world remains shapeless chaos until the artist develops what he calls "configurations in chaos," tangible and understandable forms to what she sees. As we give

Our words also determine how we view the nature of existence, that is, how we explain and understand this remarkable universe in which we find ourselves. From the time of their appearance on this planet, people have used words, in some form, to analyze (consider, again, the definition of the Sanskrit word for grammar) and consider who they are and why they are living and existing in this world. They observed, they concluded; they looked, they discussed; they pondered, they explored, they found.

And they described. They used words to define what they saw, to relate what they decided, to give substance to and share what they believed they had come to understand and learn about their lives and the world in which they live them. Although had they not had words they would have still seen and experienced the world, they would not have had any way to constitute, define, or meaningfully communicate what they saw. Yes, they could use sign language, and yes, they could use gestures, but even those are a form of word and language. Words, in some form, are essential to a meaningful world.[17]

Indeed, even though animals who, as we observed, outside of mythology and fantasy (and parakeets and some aquatic mammals whom researchers think may in fact, given certain conditions, speak[18]), do not seem to speak in

---

definition to our world with words, in the broadest sense, so the artist uses a form of "language" to formulate her perception. On this, see *The Portfolios of Ansel Adams* (Boston: Little, Brown, and Company, 1977, 1981).

17   To wit, fantasy writer George MacDonald often observed that the purpose of fantasy is not so much to convey a meaning but to awaken a meaning. What we see may be much different than what we make what we see become.

18   Specifically, a number of researchers are working on a device which they think will enable them to communicate, in some way, with dolphins. Also, scientists have known for years that whales and dolphins, among

human words, they nonetheless process (as we also observed) with images or something approximating them, things and somethings that they see and experience as they move across the planet. They process and digest the world into meaningful packets of information for their use. They must: the creature who fails to process its world is a creature that, whether by violence, apathy, or attrition, is destined to soon leave it. Bottom line, *all* sentient creatures, animal or human (despite all studies that have been done on the genetic and material similarities between animal and human, none have conclusively established that animals (that is, non-human entities) and humans are precisely the same types of beings[19]), employ some type of communicative process to grapple with, connect to, and encounter the world. To repeat, words or, perhaps better put, language, defined in the broadest sense, are essential to meaningful and sustainable existence.

Indeed, without words, we, and all other sentient beings, are magnificent creations of tremendous potential with essentially nowhere to go. If we have no way to define our world, if we have no way to express our experience of the world, if we have no way to share our perception of the world, we become like ghosts in a graveyard, vigorous enough perhaps (think

---

other aquatic animals, engage in a form of aural communication with each other. For more, see the article by MacGregor Campbell in *New Scientist*, May 9, 2011, as well as Kathleen Dudzinski, *Dolphin Mysteries: Unlocking the Secrets of Communication* (New Haven: Yale University, 2008), and Diana Reiss, *The Dolphin in the Mirror: Exploring Dolphin Minds and Saving Dolphin Lives* (New York: Houghton Mifflin Harcourt, 2011).

19   Numerous studies have demonstrated that although humans and animals, particularly chimpanzees, share a great deal of genetic material, they diverge on the final percent or so, and it is this final percent or so that makes all the difference. On the other hand, refer to the recent documentary "Project Nim" for a more tragic perspective on this dichotomy, the story of a chimpanzee whom researcher tried, from a social and linguistic standpoint, to make a human.

about the movie *Ghostbusters!*[20]), but incapable of genuinely knowing or meaningfully understanding anything around us. Even the Who's blind, deaf, and dumb "Tommy" could form pictures, pictures that perhaps only he understood, but pictures which were nonetheless portraits or reflections of his world. Likewise, the famous Helen Keller, though she could not hear or see, learned, through signs and gestures, to speak. We are made, designed, and equipped to understand and process our world.[21]

And to process our world, we need words.

(The other part of this is that the world is designed to be a place in which those who live in it may find, establish, and describe meaningful experiences. But we will address this later.)

Before she passed away a few years ago, my mother-in-law had been fading, physically as well as mentally. She heard what we said to her, but she could not verbalize her response. Her face indicated that her brain was processing what she saw and heard, but nothing came out of her mouth. But words were working in her. She was not totally without thought or image. She continued to experience the world. Only if her brain had stopped working, only if her brain had ceased to digest and evaluate the world around her, only if her brain had stopped using words, and only if her mind had stopped assessing, with words, the larger implications of what she experienced, would she no longer be. To the very end, she was interacting with her world. Granted, she already knew words, but even if she had not, even if she had been a child who lived less than twenty-four hours, as the child of a friend

---

20   See the 1984 movie (along with its 1989 sequel, *Ghostbusters II*) of the same name (Sony Pictures).

21   We refer here to the famous "rock opera" released in 1969 by Decca Records. For information on Helen Keller, see her memoir, *The Story of My Life* (New York: Doubleday, 1954).

of mine unfortunately did, she would still have been in some way processing what she experienced. She was never mute inside *and* out.

Our lives would not be the existence that we understand and experience on a moment by moment basis unless words or, to speak more broadly, the fact of communicability and speech, were not, potentially, anyway, present. Because we live, we communicate, and because we communicate we express the fact of our existence, the fact of our presence and experience, and the truth that we have form, meaning, and a vision beyond the present moment. Our ability to communicate shapes and propels our world.[22]

Our ability to communicate also indicates that we have a sense of self-awareness and purpose. Because we communicate, because we have the ability to formulate and express thoughts as speech, we have the ability to view ourselves from outside of ourselves, to think about ourselves and what we are doing with our lives. We are aware that we exist; we are aware that we are aware that we are here, and we are aware that we can manipulate the circumstances and contingencies of our existence. Also, we are able to consider the future, to see ourselves in a realm beyond the immediate moment, to align the present time with another as yet to come time ahead. We are aware of more than the passing demarcation of space and time. With this, we can develop meaningful responses to our perception that we, life, and the world change, and that we can construct various ways to deal with these eventualities, ways to continue existing with hope, joy, and meaning. And we do all this with speech. Speech (communication) enables us to see ourselves as we

---

22 As Steven Pinker puts it in his *The Language Instinct: How The Mind Creates Language* (New York: Harper Perennial, 1994): "Language is so tightly woven into human experience that it is scarcely impossible to imagine life without it."

are now as well as what and where we hope we might one day be. Speech allows us to know that we can determine our destiny. It invites us to know that, to draw a page from the philosopher and commentator Ayn Rand, we can always strive for individual greatness in the reality that we inherit and create.[23]

Again, if we did not have words, if we did not have some capacity to communicate, and the ability, in varying degrees, to engage the world in a meaningful and conscious way, we would have no reason, no framework, and no impetus to be. We would be essentially dead in the water.

Now this doesn't mean that we will not experience the world without words to describe it, or that the world will not disclose itself to us without us having words to define it. Any animal can tell us that. It does mean, however, that every sentient creature has a way to put definition to what it sees and experiences. It has a way to make sense of what it processes as it moves in its reality. For the human species, the marvelous concoction which we call *homo sapiens,* this way is in words, expressed orally, in written form, or both. What humans see, what humans experience, what they discover and find, they do so with words, words with which they put their perceptions into forms and shapes meaningful to them. Again, we are not saying that an experience is not meaningful without words to define it; merely that words, be they pictures, images, or syllabic expressions are the means that we use to know and understand that we are experiencing it.[24]

---

23   For more on Ayn Rand, see the most recently published biography of her, *Ayn Rand and the World She Made,* by Anne Conover Heller (New York: Nan A. Talese/Doubleday, 2009).

24   We think here of the religious mystic, who often has experiences which she cannot readily put into words. See Evelyn Underhill, *Mysticism* (New York: Doubleday, 1990), and Ann Taves, *Religious Experience Reconsidered* (Princeton, New Jersey: Princeton, 2009).

This even applies to delusions and hallucinations: those who experience and report them always do so with words. Indeed, with apologies to the British philosopher John Locke and his famous notion of *tabula rasa* ("blank slate"), even a baby has a way to make sense of what she experiences. Everyone has a way to formulate meaning from what she sees and experiences. And everyone does this with words—language and speech—in the broadest sense.[25]

So words really do bring the world to us. They ensure that we are beings and that we are beings who know that they experience a world. Moreover, though words reveal what we already know, they also reveal what we may not know about what we think we already know. They affirm, but they also enlarge and expand. Words are the progenitors of discovery as much as they are the describers of it. Words ground and describe what we believe to be real and true, and yet words also create what we might *want* to be real and true. Our words are the springboard of our world, in all its nearly infinite dimensions, past, present, and the future to come.

Or as George Orwell observes in his novel *1984*, his profound explication of the ominous character of the totalitarian state, one of the most dangerous things that humans can do is to "shrink" language, to make it smaller than what it is or smaller than what it ought to be. For the longer that we "shrink" language, Orwell noted, the "smaller" it becomes, and soon is of no use at all. Humanity, we therefore might infer, is only as big as it allows its language to be. Words make us whom we are.[26]

If words are indeed all of these things, then we must also

---

25   See Locke's *An Essay Concerning Human Understanding,* edited by Alexander Campbell Fraser (New York: Barnes and Noble Books, 2004).

26   See George Orwell, *1984* (New York: Harcourt, Brace and Company, 1949).

assume that words, as we observed when we thought about Adam and Eve, convey emotion. The Swiss-born philosopher Jean Jacques Rousseau (1712-1778) once remarked that the emergence of speech, which he defined as intelligible verbal communication, came about as a result of passion. People, he argued, began not by reasoning but by feeling, by feeling through the passions which they all shared.[27]

Although modern psychology has proven Rousseau wrong (thought always precedes emotion), his point is nonetheless worth considering here. Unless we are always and everywhere thoroughly rational beings (in practice, a foolish assumption to make!) then words represent not only intelligent communication, speech, and revelation, but passion, the passion of love and imagination, of quest and creation, the passion that drives people to dream and envision beyond the present and immediate, the passion that fuels countless invention and intrigue, the passion that inspires the ultimate artistic moment. Words express our innate thirst for existence, our perennial and profound longing to be fully human.

We can then say that words are the integrating points of our knowing *and* being, the expression of our intellect as well as of our heart. They are as much feeling as they are verbal articulations of it. In words we see the comprehensive definer and expression of human experience, the emotional and mental fullness of how people see the world, the passions, imaginings, dreams, feelings, and speech of the human species. Words define, words ignite, and words express our passion about our experience. Words are all.[28]

---

27   So he puts it in chapter two of his *Essay on the Origin of Languages,* edited, translated, and annotated by Victor Gourevitch (New York: Harper and Row, 1986).

28   We might also think here of the ancient Hebrew way of looking at the heart (*leb*). For the ancient Hebrew, the heart constituted not

In addition, because we speak, be it with mind or heart, we understand that we are inherently personal beings. We are not opaque points without sensitivity, intelligence, or feeling, but highly personal beings who engage and interact with each other and the world. Humans are not rocks. We speak because we are personal, a fact that we demonstrate whenever we speak.

This neat and ordered equation, however, has another part to it. As we noted earlier, we would only think to communicate if living in the world was a communicative experience, if the world was something that we could explore, experience, discover, and inhabit in a meaningful way. Otherwise, although we may be communicative beings, we may as well not be beings at all. It would be like living in a blank space: though we may think that we know we were here, how would we know, for where would we really be? We would be able only to describe ourselves (and even this is a question mark), to ourselves, and even this would have no meaning because we would have no way to determine who we are.

For instance, think about Tom Hanks in the movie *Cast Away* and the "relationship" he established with a face he drew on a volleyball, a face he called Wilson. He could not live without engaging in some form of communication. No one can (even a hermit must, at least on occasion, think to herself). Now suppose that Hank's desert island was constructed such that he could not experience it, much less talk about it. What would he be able to do?[29]

Well, you may say, he still has words. He can still speak.

---

merely the physical organ on the left side of a human body, but the total expression of a thinking person's being. Similarly, properly employed, words, or language in some form, can convey everything about us and our experience.

29 See the movie, released in 2000 by Dreamworks and Twentieth Century Fox.

True, but what if he had nothing to speak about? What if he could not experience what was around him? What if the desert island had no information to disclose? It would be like staring into a blank wall, like living in a box: he would not know whether anything was really there. Hanks's brain would have nothing to process, for there would be nothing to experience. All he could do is think about what he *couldn't* think about, a self-defeating eventuality. He would not even be able to conclude, as did René Descartes, that if he can think, he must definitely exist: he wouldn't even know that he is somewhere to exist. He would know he is, but whom and where would he be?

This is a recipe for insanity. We can only be communicative beings in a communicative universe, a universe that enables discovery, description, and speech. Merely thinking of words is not enough. We must be able to, in some way, to experience our world. If our words are to have any substance, point, or value, we must be able to know and understand and experience that the world is a place of insight, opportunity, and discovery. We must know that the world will speak.[30]

Clearly, if the universe did not speak (not necessarily verbally but in a way that makes it comprehensible to our finite minds), if the universe were not a place that could be experienced, we would not speak or experience, either. We would be vacuums, bereft of explanation for ourselves and no reason to seek it, no reason as to why we were here, no way to know *how* we got here. Reality would be a mirage, totally devoid of content and explanation. Oddly enough and

---

30 This is why solitary confinement is so debilitating: the prisoner is totally cut off from all human contact, a condition which, as a quick look at America's maximum security prison in the mountains of Colorado demonstrates, can eventually drive her quite mad. See "Tortured by Solitude" by Sarah Shourd in *The New York Times,* November 6, 2011.

as contradictory as it sounds, everything would be nothing. And nothing never produces anything.

The world speaks. The world is constantly functioning and expressing and sharing something we didn't know previously. It's always new to us. The world is designed, bent, and destined to disclose itself, to make itself known, and we are similarly designed, bent, and destined to know it, to make the world known to us in our lives. We are made to seek out the universe, for the universe exists to be known. It's not a static object. It speaks.[31]

And it speaks in ways that we had not known beforehand. Because the universe is constantly producing newness, we in turn constantly experience newness, constantly uncovering new facets of possibility for our lives. We live according to what the world reveals to us, whether this is something we find or something that, in some way, finds us. Moreover, even if we believe or feel that we have found nothing—and vice versa—we in fact have already found something. Eventually, somehow and some way, we find. Though we may not find fully, we nonetheless find, even if we find that we cannot find. For in a world in which finding is possible, this is to find as well. We live by what we discover, perceive, experience, and see before us. We are communicative and processing beings who live in a communicative and constantly changing and processing universe.[32]

For instance, do you ever *not* wonder about what you don't know? Or do you ever *not* think about will come next? Or do you ever *not* imagine what may exist beyond what you

---

31   As Benjamin Meyers puts it in his "On Taking Communion with My Students" in his collection of poems, *Elegy for Trains* (New York: Village Books, 2011), "the world is text." It is always speaking.

32   Put another way, the world is revelation. We will discuss this more later, but for now consider revelation to be something that has not been previously experienced or seen.

see? Of course not: as Aristotle observed long ago, we all are creatures that seek to know.[33]

We think about such things because we are purposeful and communicative beings who are living in a purposeful and communicative universe. If we were not, we would not be here, nor would we be who we are. If we did not wonder, we would not be human. And part of wondering is believing that there is something to wonder about, that there are mysteries we do not know, that there are unknowns we cannot immediately fathom, that there are things we do not or cannot see but which we believe, or think we believe, might be there. Part of wondering is believing that there is an unknown waiting to be found and, subsequently, to be known. To wonder is to believe, and to believe is to accept the fact of a communicative universe, a disclosing cosmos. It is to acknowledge that the universe speaks, to believe that it communicates itself. It is to believe in the certainty of newness and continually unfolding possibility.[34]

We are communicative and personal beings who live in a communicative universe which we process and experience and express with language, with words and speech. We are beings who wonder, beings who ponder, beings who always want to know more and, perhaps most important, beings who are aware that we do so. We are also beings who speak about what we wonder about. We almost always have something to say.

---

33   So goes the first line of Aristotle's *Metaphysics*, as translated by W. D. Ross in *The Complete Works of Aristotle,* edited by Jonathan Barnes (Princeton: Princeton University Press, 1984).

34   We might draw a page here from the novelist George MacDonald, who famously observed that the "purpose of fantasy was not to *convey* a meaning but *awake* a meaning." By its very nature, the world is designed to "awaken" meaning in us, to ignite, as we watch, the truth and purpose that it intrinsically contains. See Alan Jacobs, "The Ghost Writer: Walking with Ian Sinclair" in *Books and Culture,* November-December 2011.

Let's return to Adam and Eve. We observed that Adam and Eve learned about and defined the world with words. Adam and Eve, as do we, lived in a communicative universe. But why? Why do we speak? Why can we speak? Why do we live in a communicative universe, a universe that speaks to us, that grants us time and space to formulate and pursue meaning and purpose? Why are we personal beings who speak in a speaking universe?

These are massive questions. Clearly, we know that this world is a world built upon words and, in some larger form, speech. We experience this every day. We also know that communication is necessary, essential, and real. Would the Ainur ever have spoken if they had not been designed to do so and spoken to, if they had not been living in a world in which communication was a possibility? It's highly unlikely.

Some years ago, a book, *If You are Afraid of the Dark, Remember the Night Rainbow,* appeared on some of the nation's bookshelves. A highly fanciful book, it is full of interesting *non sequiturs.* One of them goes like this: "If the birds forget their songs, listen to a pebble instead." Do pebbles talk? Most geologists will tell us that, despite the Seventies craze about "pet rocks," rocks do not speak. They are thoroughly inanimate objects. A world of rocks is a world of verbal silence.[35]

Ours, however, is not a world of silence. It is always speaking. Our world is a cacophony of sound. Yet if our world is this way, a world of movement and sound, of living beings, living beings who communicate and commune with each other, where did it and communication and speech come from? How did the world come to be, how did the world come to develop the capacity to communicate? How did we

---

35   See Cooper Eden's *If You are Afraid of the Dark, Remember the Night Rainbow* (San Francisco: Chronicle Books, 1979).

develop the capacity to communicate? Furthermore, as we have observed, if communication involves personality, in some form, then this is a personal world, a world in which personality and emotion and passion, variously experienced and expressed, drive every living being. And where did these come from? It seems difficult to accept that purpose and personality and communication came out of impersonal and lifeless plasma, the proverbial layers of primordial cosmic rocks and dust basic to nearly every modern cosmological schemata of origins. It seems difficult to imagine that words and speech emerged from a wordless universe or a mute antediluvian substance.

Put another way, why are we personal and communicative beings who use words and speech with definition and purpose?

To answer these questions, we will not look at science, at least not directly, nor will we look at psychology, at least not immediately. Both of these disciplines are important and both provide critical insights into who we are. But neither science nor psychology tells us what we, personal and communicative beings, mean. Neither will explain to us *why* we are or why we are here. And understanding why we are and why we are here is essential to understanding why we are personal and why we communicate. Science and psychology will talk to us about the mechanics of meaning, but they do not always provide insight into the meaning of meaning, the reason *for* meaning. They do not always explain why. If the world is built upon words, upon speech, and if words define, circumscribe, and relate meaning, then we should try to understand why, where, and how words began. Maybe then we will see what life really means.

For this reason, we will look at a religious text (for religions are usually where we find clues to ultimate meaning), a religious text which, we will see, carries enormous implications for the way we are today. It is a text which will allow us to see why we are personal. It is also a text that will enable us to think about why and how communication is so important in our lives. In addition, it is a text that will give us clearer insight into that from which we came, the essence and meaning of our origins. It will help us to see the meaning of the *Urstoff*, the "stuff" of the world in which we now live and, as the ancient Greek Stoic Aratus (as he is quoted in the chapter seventeen of the Bible's Book of Acts) puts it, "have our being."

This text is from the Bible, the New Testament, the Gospel of John.

Before we dig into the text, let's present the first few verses on which we will focus:

> "In the beginning was the Word, and the Word was with God, and the Word was God. He was in the beginning with God. All things came into being through Him, and apart from Him nothing came into being that has come into being. In Him was life and the life was the light of humanity." (John 1:1-4).[36]

"In the beginning was the Word." With these words, John begins his gospel (a word meaning, literally, "good news"), his account of the life and teachings of Jesus. Like its Synoptic (from Greek words meaning, "to see with") counterparts, the gospels of Matthew, Mark, and Luke, John's rendering of Jesus' time on earth represents his perception and recollection

---

36   Unless otherwise stated, all scripture verses come from the New American Standard translation of the Biable (The Lockman Foundation) (Grand Rapids: Zondervan, 1960, 2000).

of the events to which he, as one of Jesus' twelve apostles, had been an eyewitness for the roughly three years of Jesus' earthly ministry. Unlike a history book written in our present day, studded with copious documentation and volumes of footnotes, John's recounting does not claim to be a complete picture of everything Jesus said and did (indeed, he notes in the last verse of his gospel that, "and there are also many other things which Jesus did, which if they were written in detail, I suppose that even the world itself would not contain the books that would be written"). Rather, it is John's compilation of those phenomena and recountings about Jesus which he deemed most relevant and important to the people of his day, the millions of people strewn about the massive Roman Empire in which he lived. Out of all the episodes that marked Jesus' life, John wrote about those which he believed would speak most clearly to this diverse range of people of who Jesus was and what he accomplished in his short time on the earth.

Let's repeat the initial phrase: "In the beginning was the Word."

What is John saying? Note first that the word translated as "beginning" is the Greek word "αρχη." A cognate of αρχω, "to rule" or to "begin," αρχη almost always signifies primacy, be it in time or rank. It marks a fundamental starting point, a point which has no precursors or predecessors, a starting point before which nothing else was, a point that was present before everything else began or came to be. Αρχη represents an absolute and categorical beginning. Nothing precedes it.

By absolute beginning, we mean that αρχη is not just a point in time, be it a birth, the first month of a calendar year, or the start of a new semester of school. All of these have antecedent beginnings, chronological contexts in which they take place. They do not occur in a vacuum, nor do they occur without another event occurring before them. They are dependent on and flow out of a physical past, the real and, in some sense, verifiable train of events that precedes them. They require history, a span of material time, short or long, in order to be. The beginnings which they mark are merely new twists on or developments of old news. A birth follows gestation; the first month follows the last day of the previous month; the new semester of school follows the last day of summer. In every case, what is "new" emerged out of an "old."

It is not so with αρχη. Αρχη is a beginning that, paradoxically, is without a beginning. It does not require an antecedent, nor is it contingent upon previous history to happen. Nothing need occur for αρχη to be. Αρχη can "be" before or apart from anything else that is. Nothing need be present and nothing need have happened for αρχη to be.

In other words, αρχη is a beginning without a beginning. It has always been.

How can this be? We can think of two possibilities. One, αρχη is a beginning which, for whatever reason, suddenly pops out of nothing, thrusting itself, somehow, some way into existence. Without any warning, perhaps without any reason, it appears, mysterious and without cause, either creating other things or, alternatively, inserting itself into whatever cosmic substance may be there to receive it.

Yet if this is the case, αρχη has a beginning. Regardless of how it began, it nonetheless began. If αρχη is indeed the absolutely absolute beginning, the beginning before which all other beginnings come, however, it should not even begin at all. Nothing, not even "nothingness" itself, should enable it to be. In truth, if αρχη comes out of any sort of substance, be it cosmic or even otherworldly, we must question whether it really began on its own. How do we know whether this "substance" did not in some way birth or at least provide the conditions under which αρχη came to life or into existence? Whether αρχη appears *in* something, or whether it has come *out of* something, the point remains that it would be dependent on something else for its existence. And if it depends on something else for its existence, then it could not be the uncaused beginning: by the nature of what it is (if we can even use the word "is" here), an uncaused beginning has no cause.

Also, if αρχη came from something, where did that something come from? And where did the something from which this something came come from? And on and on we go: it is the age old problem of infinite regress. We will never know the ultimate beginning.

Let's consider the other possibility. This is that αρχη had no beginning, that is, it has always been, that it really is an uncaused cause. In a word, αρχη is eternal: it had no beginning, and it will have no end. Αρχη denotes a beginning which never really began. It is a beginning that has always been there, because it has never *not* been there. It is also a beginning that will have no ending, because it never really began. It is the beginning of all beginnings, yet, oddly, it has no beginning, and it is the end of all ends, although, oddly enough, it has no end. It has always been, and it always will be. It has always existed.

This is difficult to swallow. How can something never begin, yet always be? How can something with no beginning somehow *be,* indeed *always* be, always be alive and living, never being born yet never dying, either? The thought should strain any normal person's notion of credulity and what is physically possible. How can something never start, yet always be going—and never end?

Before we try to answer these questions, let's remind ourselves about whom we are. Let's remind ourselves that we are creatures of finitude. We are limited and ultimately terminal (no matter how hard we try, one day, regardless of how long we may live, we all will die). Also, as the German philosopher Immanuel Kant pointed out long ago, our little minds cannot look at life or existence without thinking of them in terms of causation, space, and time. We are born with an inherent propensity to look at our world as something that one, functions with a process of cause and effect, that is, everything has a cause, a reason for it to happen; two, functions in a tangible and definable space on a globe with a definite and limited form; and three, is subject to a continuum of time, a continuum in which things begin and things end. If you don't believe this, test Kant: try to think of the world without any of these things. You'll never succeed. We are now and forever creatures of finitude, of causation, space, and time. We expect starts and finishes, and beginnings and endings: we cannot imagine things not beginning and, although we may sometimes want something to never end, we cannot imagine, fully, something that never ends.[37]

Think also of Isaac Newton's conclusions about physical reality. For every action, he asserted, there is an equal and opposite reaction. Every cause has an effect, and every effect is a potential cause. The universe is a playground of cause and effect. If cause and effect did not exist, neither would the universe. Although we may not think about this often, we implicitly assume it. It is part of who we are as human beings.[38]

Hence, we engage in the world, exploring, communicating, and being, always, whether we are conscious of it or not, doing so in this framework of cause and effect, set as it is in a larger

---

37 For a very technical look at Kant's reasoning, see his massive *Critique of Pure Reason*, translated by Norman Kemp Smith (New York: Macmillan, 1965).

38 See Newton's conclusions as he presented them in his ground breaking *Principia: Mathematical Principles of Natural Philosophy*, as translated, fairly recently, by Andrew Motte (New York: Prometheus, 1995).

perceptual compass of space and time. We are naturally prone to seek out our borders and boundaries, origins and destinies, and beginnings and endings, to consider and grapple with all things in the shadow of our given faculty of cause and effect and our apperceptions of space and time. We investigate and apprehend life's meanings as a function of origin (cause) and destiny (effect).

Why do we want to know "why"? We want to know "why" because we think in terms of cause and effect. We want to know "why" because we do not understand why this cause (the world) is the way it is, and because we do not always want to accept or believe in the reasonableness of the effects that this cause has produced or bequeathed to us. We may not like that we do not always know "why," but we understand that we cannot live without asking the question. We cannot live without cause and effect, and we cannot live without an idea of space and time.

This is why we find John's picture of αρχη so difficult to grasp. Our minds are not designed to think about things outside the reach of causation, space, and time. When we try to make them do so, we end up bursting our categories of what we otherwise consider to be real, reasonable, and true. In order to talk about αρχη as a beginning and end without beginning and end, we must therefore think about it by using the language of eternity.

What's eternity? Briefly, we can say that eternity is a state of endlessness, a state of endlessness that never began and which will never end. It always "is." Though it generates beginnings and ends, eternity is neither, for it never really began, nor will it ever really end. Again, it simply "is."

Αρχη is eternal. It is the root and foundation of all things, but it itself never really began. Nothing caused it, and nothing can materially affect it. Αρχη will "be" whether or not anything else ever comes to be.

If you are still having problems accepting this, consider the alternative: the universe suddenly and unexpectedly popped out of nothing. Granted, this is what much of modern cosmology insists happened. Their theories for how this could be range from the presence of multi-universes, the existence of antimatter, the fact of unattached gravity (a difficult proposition in itself[39]), and more. All of these ideas, however, assume the presence of something, be it a fact, law, point, or presence that preceded everything else and from which everything else came. And where did *these* things come from? We have no answer.

Either way we go, we are faced with the same conundrum. Where did the first "thing" come from? How did *it* begin? As long as we think in these categories (which, as we observed, it is our natural propensity to do), we will face a problem of origins. Even if we definitively and conclusively identified the absolutely original substance (the "Urstoff") from which all other substances came, we would still be left with trying to figure out how *it* came to be. We would still want and need to determine and establish a starting point. It's part of our humanness.[40]

---

39   Even gravity cannot come to be without something within and around which it moves and functions. Without this, it means nothing. Without something, gravity is nothing, in the truest sense of the word. It would simply not be. For a counter to this thought, see famous cosmologist Stephen Hawkings's latest book, *The Grand Design* (New York: Bantam, 2010), as well as Lawrence M. Krauss's *A Universe from Nothing* (New York: Free Press, 2012) and its thoughts on "virtual particles," objects which, although they do not actually exist, nonetheless do, and consequently endow empty space with mass. However, where did this space come from?

40   Or the "original substance," that which the earliest philosophers, the Pre-Socratics, sought to understand. See Kirk, G. S., Raven, J. E., and Schofield, M., *The Presocratic Philosophers,* Second Edition (Cambridge: Cambridge University, 1957, 1983).

Therefore, crazy as it seems, perhaps it really is best, when we think about cosmic origins, to assume the existence of something which has always existed, something which has always been around, something which, in some way unfathomable to us, just "is." This "something" will exist without any outside agency or support and, as difficult as this may seem, require no help to be, for it always was (or is: that's the nature of eternity). All things considered, this seems to be the only fair and logical conclusion to draw. We can of course respond that we do not see how this can possibly be right and that we intend to keep working on the problem, but this is simply a ploy to avoid coming to grips with the inevitable. To wit, if we wish to insist that there was a definite beginning, we must still explain how it is here, how it itself appeared, and how it itself came out of nothing. These all are essentially insuperable challenges which leave us with little or no wiggle room. Clearly, nothing can come out of nothing.

Moreover, insisting on, against all logic and evidence, a non-eternal beginning, leaves unanswered the ultimate question: why? Why are we and the world here? But we will address this later.

We therefore elect to embrace αρχη as a beginning which in fact is not a beginning: an eternity.

As we shall soon explore in greater detail, however, if we embrace this assertion, we must also assume that αρχη as the absolute beginning cannot be a form of impersonal matter, that is, earth, cosmic dust, or primordial plasma, as some of the ancient Greek writers wanted to make it.[41] This

---

41 So does Hesiod observe in his *Theogony* that "Chaos was first of all … ". Even Hesiod had to assume the presence of something, something that was perhaps always there, that preceded everything else. See *Theogony*, translated by Dorothea Wender (New York: Penguin Books, 1973). Another example is the creation story from Egyptian theology, which states that in the beginning there was "Ptah, who gave life to all the

would force us to argue that something that does not even know that it exists (does a rock know it exists?!) somehow made everything else exist. This would demand that we in turn answer the question of where would impersonal matter, matter that does not talk or think, come from? Why is it here? How did it get here? How would something that could not think about itself or create itself come to be here? What would be the point?[42]

Nonetheless, eternal beginning or not, we are still left with an enigma: how do we begin to know where everything came from? If we try to address this question meaningfully, we must realize that we are dealing with things that, try as we might, we will simply never be able to resolve and grasp fully. Time and time again, we will bump against the limits of our knowing. So what are we to do?

We must learn to think in terms of paradox. We must learn to embrace things that do not seem to fit together, things that do not appear to align cleanly, but things which, if we are sufficiently wise and honest with ourselves, we admit that, even if we do not wish to, we must nonetheless accept. As Blaise Pascal noted long ago, we must accept the limits of our reason.[43] We must accede to conclusions which may explain in part, but not in full, conclusions which, as the theologian

---

gods." Like Hesiod, this writer recognizes that there had to be something from which all things began. See the reconstructed text in *Ancient Near Eastern Texts, op cit.*

42   As Admiral Richard E. Byrd observed in the diary that he kept during his early twentieth century solo sojourn in Antarctica, the universe is too orderly and complete to be a product of blind chance: there must be purpose. And purpose, as we are noting, cannot come from an impersonal beginning. It's impossible. See Byrd's *Alone: The Classic Polar Adventure* (New York: Kodansha, 1938, 1995).

43   Pascal, Blaise, *Pensées and Other Writings* (Oxford: Oxford University, 1990).

Wolfhart Pannenberg puts it, are "contrary to experience by *exceeding its capacity*"[44] (italics mine). Again, this reflects the demands and constructs of our humanness: we will never understand everything as it actually is (a fact which Immanuel Kant pointed out as well[45]). Logic, as Cardinal John Henry Newman argued toward the close of the nineteenth century, has its limits.[46]

For finite creatures living in a finite reality and searching for meaning, real and genuine meaning in that finite reality, paradox is inevitable.

Αρχη is such a paradox. It is a beginning which never really began, a beginning which required nothing to be, for it has always been. Yet αρχη is a beginning which, if we hope to develop a credible picture of global origins, we cannot do without. We need αρχη to make sense of our origins. As odd as it seems, we need an uncaused beginning to explain our own "caused" beginning. Can we who have a beginning really explain why we are here? We need a beginning which nothing else can claim *it* began, a beginning without cause and beyond effect, a beginning which never really began.

We need an αρχη, an infinite and eternal αρχη.[47]

Before we go on, let us remind ourselves once more

---

44   See Wolfhart Pannenberg, *Jesus—God and Man* (London: SCM Press, 1967)

45   See, again, Kant's monumental *Critique of Pure Reason.*

46   John Henry Newman, *Essay in Aid of a Grammar of Assent* (South Bend: University of Notre Dame, 1992).

47   Understand that eternity and infinity are not the same thing. Eternity describes something in relation to time whereas infinity describes a concept of space as well as of time (although as John D. Barrow points out in his *The Infinite Book* (New York: Pantheon, 2005), given the idea of infinity, we finite beings cannot conceive of an infinite space and infinite time for we would need an infinite amount of time to do so!). We will return to eternity and infinity in greater detail later.

that we are creatures of finitude who inhabit three and four dimensions in a universe with, according to cosmologists, at least ten more. We have limits. We have boundaries. We simply cannot grasp the idea of eternity, cannot grasp the notion of an experience outside of our earthly experience of momentary movement and passage. Try as we might, we cannot fathom how something has always existed.[48]

Nor can we comprehend the idea of infinity. We cannot fathom how something can "be" indefinitely and without measure beyond and outside of time, how something can have no boundaries or limits on its capacity to sustain, present, or generate itself or anything else within it. Although we try to imagine how such a thing can be, we simply cannot take hold of it fully. Our puny cause and effect finite minds are not equipped to do so.

Yet we must admit that this doesn't mean that such things do not exist, or that we do not experience them. Can we prove that there is no eternity? Can we prove that there is no infinity? In both cases, we cannot. In fact, we constantly validate the existence of eternity and infinity in our daily experience. How many of us have not imagined that there exists another realm of experience beyond our own? How many of us have not wondered what is beyond her, or pondered what she cannot see but which she is convinced is there? How many of us have not dreamed about living forever? How many of us have longed for something, something wonderful and amazing, to go on indefinitely, to never end? How many of us have wanted to find something, an idea, experience, or something else with endless possibilities, something with an endless number of options for our use and pleasure?

---

48   Realize that when we talk about existing in the context of eternity, we are not talking about existence in the sense that you and I exist, but a state of existence beyond our own

Who indeed? There is no one on this planet who can unequivocally claim that she has not, at least once, considered such things.[49] It is human to wonder, it is human to think about what might be. It is entirely human to wonder about the metaphysical ("big nature," a term which we will discuss more later), to cultivate a sense of bigness, endlessness, and infinity, be it directed toward this life or one that may lay beyond it. Otherwise, we may as well be rocks and gravel. Once again, we quote Aristotle: we all wish to know.[50]

Moreover, whether we believe this bigger picture to be physical or something else does not matter. The point is that whether it is simply the thought that we can experience something more than what we are experiencing in the present moment; the idea that, try as we might, we will probably never completely grasp the nature of who we are; or a simple sense of humility, the belief, honestly stated, that we are infinitesimally small beings in an infinitely large cosmos, we all admit to a sense of mystery, a sense that some dimensions of our understanding lie beyond our immediate ken.[51]

---

49   Indeed, even Friedrich Nietzsche, no friend of religious transcendence, positioned his "overman" as one who seeks his meaning continually and without end in an eternity of earthly existence, an "infinity of nothing." See his *Beyond Good and Evil*, translated by Walter Kaufmann in *Basic Writings of Friedrich Nietzsche* (New York: Modern Library, 1995), and *The Gay Science*, translated by Walter Kaufmann (New York: Random House, 1974).

50   For multiple reflections on this longing for a "more" beyond this life, check *The Book of Heaven*, co-authored by Carol Zaleski and Philip Zaleski (New York: Oxford, 2000).

51   Even if we draw a page from the mental reductionists and insist that we are no more than chemicals, we still have not really explained *why* we are the way we are. Chemicals may explain how, but they do not explain why. For more on reductionism, check John Heil, *Philosophy of Mind* (London: Routledge, 1998) and Arnold H. Modell, *Imagination and the Meaningful Brain* (Cambridge, Massachusetts: MIT, 2006).

Further, even if we do not attach any spiritual or religious significance to these longings, we are nonetheless naturally bent to think about existence in the umbra of them, to pursue our lives in the context of some sort of infinity and eternity (however we define them). To do so is to be fully honest, as well as fully human.

Also, as we have observed, regardless of our religious orientation, we are hard pressed to imagine or explain our origins (and therefore ourselves) if we did not have a thought of something bigger than we, something that we did not create, something that in some way framed or even birthed the universe in which we live. Our sense of the infinite and causation demands it. Whether we think about origins in terms of divine creation, the Big Bang, or something in between them, we find origins difficult, if not impossible to explain unless we can invoke an event, power, or circumstance we do not make. We all need a bigger picture, of some kind, to make sense of our world. That is how we are made. As Alfred North Whitehead put it,

"Our minds are finite, and yet even in the circumstances of finitude we are

> surrounded by possibilities that are infinite,
> and the purpose of life is to grasp as much as
> we can of that infinitude."[52]

Again, we all need an αρχη, an eternity, an infinity.[53]

---

52 See Whitehead, Alfred North, *Process and Reality*, edited by David Ray Griffin and Donald W. Sherburne (New York: Macmillan, 1929, 1978).

53 Regrettably, this fact most often rings true when we face the prospect of death, be it our own or a person we love. We instinctively feel utterly helpless, totally impotent and defenseless in the face of nonexistence. Despite all our efforts, all our science, technology, religion, and philosophy,

Even if we do not fully understand them, we must realize that we need them, that we need the paradoxes that eternity and infinity impose on our lives. In fact, we need them for more than emotional support. We also need them because the world and our perception of it cannot exist without them. Time is only time because of eternity: if we were eternal, we would not require time. But without eternity, time has no anchor, no beginning, no ending. It loses all definition.

And without definition, time, and space as well, for neither can erupt out of nothing, lose all possibility of hope. Where, really, are we? And how did anything ever begin? Without time, space cannot be.[54]

And without space, time means nothing.

Similarly, without a sense of infinity, we have no context for our finitude.[55] We need a notion of the infinite to give

---

we fail to fully penetrate the meaning of death and the full gamut of its implications for and effects on our lives and sensibilities. Regardless of what we believe about an afterlife, death remains frightfully final, an event for which we ultimately have no satisfactory, from an existential standpoint, ground of divining its purpose. So did the writer Susan Sontag, who died of myelodysplastic syndrome, a form of leukemia in 2004, announce, shortly before her death, that, "I'm going to die," then break down crying, fraught with the impending horror of non-existence. (On this, see her son David Rieff's memoir, *Swimming in a Sea of Death* (New York: Simon & Schuster, 2008)). Moreover, even though Julian Barnes's *Nothing to be Frightened of* (New York: Knopf, 2008) blithely dismisses fears and misgivings about death, it nevertheless cannot seem to completely understand or accept what death, taken at face value, that is, the absolute and irrecoverable termination of life, might mean. Death remains a dark mystery.

54   Here we may draw a page from Albert Einstein's ideas about relativity, that even if time and space remain uncertain relative to each person, they nonetheless exist. See Einstein's (edited by Robert W. Lawson) *Relativity: The Special and General Theory* (London: Really Simple Media, 1916, 2011).

55   Or as the philosopher Alain Badiou points out, an ordinal is not an ordinal unless there is a "multiple" ordinal that is "without limit,"

meaning to our finiteness. What would a finite universe be if there were no infinity in which to frame it? Limits do not arise from themselves but from something apart from them. What is a limit unless there is something beyond it?[56]

As Giordano Bruno observed in one of his dialogues, if we posit a finite world, and if this finite world is all that is, then where would *it* be (italics mine)? Or as Nicholas of Cusa noted, though the center of the universe is everywhere, its circumference is nowhere: it is infinite, an infinite that is a ground that, in turn, is a cause in itself, and therefore *has no* cause [like αρχη] (italics, Nicholas). Infinity is, as numerous mathematical observations as well as the famous Tristram Shandy Paradox attest, not only possible, but necessarily actual. Unless we assume a beginning for infinity, which we cannot, we must assume that an endlessness necessarily exists, an endlessness that ensures the possibility of the perception of endlessness that is essential to meaningful existence.[57]

---

something beyond the "void." See his *Being and Event,* translated by Oliver Felthnam (New York: Continuum, 2005).

56   On this point, consider how, by assuming the notion of a plenum, in a manner of speaking, of space, mathematics relies on the notion of infinity, for instance, the infinity of a straight line: apart from bumping into a point, it will continue indefinitely.

57   For Bruno, see his *Of Infinity, the Universe, and the World;* for de Cusa, see his *De docta ignorantia* (On Learned Ignorance). Consider as well the mathematical principle of the infinite set and its access to another infinite set as it was established by George F. L. P. Cantor in the late nineteenth century. For more, check *Infinite Ascent* by David Berlinski (London: Weidenfeld & Nicolson, 2006). Also, see William Lane Craig's observation on infinity in William L. Craig and Quentin Smith, *Theism, Atheism, and Big Bang Cosmology* (Oxford: Oxford University, 1993), specifically, that finitude will never produce infinity: it is impossible. Infinity must come from somewhere else; but because it is infinity, it cannot. Hence, it always exists.

Try as we might, we cannot imagine life without eternity and infinity.

(As a sidebar, oddly, though some of us may want to deny the existence of God or to say that God is a concept devoid of content, we find it much more difficult to deny that we at one time in our lives pondered, perhaps longed for the eternity, or at least a sense of it, that most religions believe to be implicit in God's essence. Similarly, regardless of our metaphysical (again, a term to which we will return later) commitments, we instinctively understand that properly grasping the content of the world means agreeing that at least the *idea* of infinity is necessary, even if we do not understand it. Hence, even if we doubt there is a God, we do not dispute that there is an infinite, an idea, like eternity, which is traditionally attached to him/her/it. In sum, regardless of our metaphysical beliefs, we must admit that we are hard wired, from evolution or otherwise, to think in terms of infinity and eternity.)

What does this have to do with the question of αρχη, the ultimate uncaused cause? Just this: regardless of whether we believe our origins to be material or immaterial, an event akin to the Big Bang or the product of a being like God, we nonetheless put our faith in an uncaused cause. Although we cannot fully or easily explain the idea of a cause that has always existed, that is, a cause without a cause, we also cannot reasonably explain the notion of something popping out of nothing. Either way, we are faced with admitting that we must set our conclusions about origins in the idea of an unexplainable and ultimately, like it or not, uncaused cause. Even if we cannot see or prove it, we must posit the existence of something that exists without a cause, something that is or at least seems infinite and without limits, beginning, and end, yet something that somehow germinates or constitutes the beginning of all things. There is really no other way to go. Again: we are trapped in paradox. We know that we are here, yet unless we posit the presence of something which, although we cannot see it, we believe to be here, too, we do not really know how or where we are here.

It's hard to find a way out of nothing.

To put it another way, we need to accept the necessity of a something (or somethingness), an infinite and eternal something or somethingness that is in some way outside of this finite realm, yet which in some way also enabled its existence, to explain our origins. Also, we need to accept that although this somethingness may share some characteristics with us and our finite realm, it is ultimately fundamentally unlike them. This something or somethingness would be present even if the universe was not, for it is infinite, and it is eternal which, as we observed, are the two essential underpinnings of material reality. Broadly speaking, this something or somethingness is the starting point of our physical experience. It must be: there is never nothing without something.

Where does this leave us? We have acknowledged the necessity of some sort of absolute cause, an uncaused cause from which all causes and effects come. We have also observed that this absolute cause must be infinite and eternal, that it must be a medium, condition, or presence without limits, beginning, or end. We have not, however, defined the nature of this cause, and we have not determined its precise relationship to everything else, that is, everything that is finite. We are only saying that such a presence must be present before anything else can come to be.

Before we go further, however, we need to unpack two ideas to which we alluded earlier. These ideas are transcendence and metaphysics.

So what is transcendence? And what is metaphysics? Transcendence and metaphysics point to or describe realms of experience, presence, or possibility beyond the visible experiences and tangible phenomena of this physical world. They signify what may exist but which we cannot now physically see, states of existence separate from, outside of, and not dependent on our material experience for their existence, but which nevertheless exist. In fact, as we noted earlier, the word metaphysics is drawn from two Greek words which mean literally "big nature," that is, something bigger than the natural world through which we journey every day.

There are many ways, however, of understanding transcendence and metaphysics. For some of us, transcendence is simply an experience, a particularly remarkable experience in which we feel "lifted" out of ourselves, elevated above our regular everyday experiences. We may experience transcendence when we look at the sun setting over the ocean, when we hear a singularly memorable and moving piece of music, gaze upon a striking work of art, or when we fall in love. In every instance, we feel "transported," as if in some ineffable way we have moved, emotionally, spiritually, or otherwise, over and beyond our normal experience.

For others of us, transcendence points to more than a particularly uplifting existential moment or experience. Transcendence points to and indeed is a palpable physical (in its own sense) state of being, a real and tangible realm of existence beyond our own. It has genuine substance. People who believe in God as a real and living being greater than themselves subscribe to this notion of transcendence. For instance, they say that God is as real as anything in this world, that in God transcendence has real form and presence. In God, as they see him/her/it, transcendence is entirely "there," there in the sense that you and I are entirely "here."

So it is with metaphysics. Some people will state very clearly that the idea of metaphysics is an impossibility, that there cannot possibly be anything beyond our earthly realm. Moreover, so these folks will say, we do not need the notion of metaphysics to make sense of our present reality. We can find all our hope and meaning in what we experience in the everyday gyrations of this physical existence. We do not need anything beyond it to anchor or validate our sense of form and purpose.

Others might say that although they will admit to the idea and necessity of metaphysics for constructing a reasonable view of reality, they do not need to suppose that metaphysics is a real realm of form and substance. It is a useful idea (we shall soon see that this is precisely what many Greeks of John's time thought) but has no real presence.

Still others will observe that not only is metaphysics real and necessary, but that it contains genuine substance as well. The metaphysical realm is as real as the one we enjoy here on earth. People who believe in God as a living and substantive being adopt this position. They are convinced that there exists a genuine and tangible (in a spiritual but entirely real sense) presence outside of our earthly experience.

Two views of reality, two views of looking at the world. Which one is best? We shall see that for John, transcendence and the metaphysical are entirely and physically real, as physically real as the sun whose existence we assume every day.[58] For this reason, if we are to accept anything we read in the biblical text which we are examining, we must also adopt this position. We must agree that transcendence is more than a particularly pleasurable experience or moment, that it is instead a substantive and genuine state of existence and being as real as anything we might see or hear on planet Earth. We must acknowledge that the metaphysical is not a dream, but is an established and, in part, verifiable reality. Furthermore,

---

58 When I say "assume" every day, I am thinking of people who live in the far northern reaches of the globe, people who, due to the natural axial rotation of the earth, do not see the sun at all during the darkest days of winter.

we must embrace the notion that we need the metaphysical to make proper sense of the world.

For many of us, of course, this may be too much to swallow. How can what we cannot see possibly be? How do we know that it is there? How can it be of any value?

These are highly legitimate questions. On the other hand, how do we really know for sure that we can reject such things, that we can reject the possibility of realms of existence and presence that we cannot see? How do we, finite and limited creatures that we are, know for certain, absolutely certain that there is no transcendent realm beyond this one? Absent becoming infinite and in total command of all knowledge, we really cannot say, categorically, that the transcendent does or does not exist. If we do, we are ignoring, even laughing at who we are. Yes, if the universe and our knowledge constitute a sphere with no possibility of boundaries beyond it, then we can conclude that there is indeed nothing beyond it. But how do we know even this? A sphere, say, the sphere of a universe or something smaller may be the full enclosure of itself, but as Bruno pointed out, where is it? Is it in space? If so, where is this space? And what is beyond it? Where did *that* come from?

We cannot begin to understand anything about this finite world without first assuming something beyond it. To do otherwise is to ignore the reality of beginnings. The universe had to come from *somewhere,* and the universe cannot be explained without understanding that it is indeed *somewhere,* a somewhere that in turn must be circumscribed by a larger "somewhere" in turn. There must therefore be an ultimate "somewhere" in which things find their origin and meaning. Everything needs a starting point.

To the point, as we observed earlier, something cannot come out of nothing. We cannot escape the necessity of the metaphysical and transcendent.

On this point, it is well to note that although mathematical proofs may work logically, they do not always stand up to the mysterious tangles of cosmology. Absent a definable starting point or comprehensive presence, in the big picture, even if we are able to define the world with numbers and logic, we still do not know precisely and for certain the world we are describing.[59]

Moreover, even if we say, as does many a philosopher, that statements about the transcendent have no meaning because there is no material referent that corresponds to them, we cannot dismiss them altogether. The lack of an obvious referent does not always imply nonexistence. Do we require a referent for our feelings of transcendent joy over seeing a sunset over the ocean? The ocean and sunset are there, yes, but we cannot pinpoint precisely *how* they are stirring our feelings of transcendence. We still do not have a firm anchor for explaining why we feel the way we do.[60]

Consider this: are we always, on our own, able to decide what is absolutely best for us? Do any of us ever suppose that she can live without seeking advice from others? Does anyone think that she always makes the right decisions, on her own? I would hope not. I think everyone recognizes that her perspective on herself is limited, that she cannot see everything about herself that she should see, nor can she grasp all the factors involved in a situation particular to her. Sure, we all are capable of making wise decisions, and yes, we all are able to render informed choices, but I would hope

---

59   For instance, although the Pythagoreans believed that number is the essence or "wisest" of all things, they still could not define exactly what these "things" were. For more, see, as they are cited previously, David Berlinski's *Infinite Ascent* and G. S. Kirk *et al, The Pre Socratic Philosophers*.

60   Here we think about A.J. Ayers and his many theses about these matters in his *Language, Truth, and Logic* (New York: Dover, 1946) and *Central Questions of Philosophy* (New York: William Morrow, 1973).

that none of us thinks that she never needs another's advice, instruction, or admonition. At some point, we all need a sounding board for our internal deliberations.

That, in a nutshell, is how transcendence and metaphysics function in our experience. Given our finitude and innate physical and spiritual frailty, we cannot expect to always understand everything there is to understand or to know everything there is to know. It's impossible. However, when we factor in a real transcendence and a real metaphysical, and acknowledge a larger presence, a bigger picture, a more comprehensive and universal perspective on our experience, we benefit greatly. We acknowledge that there is indeed something bigger than we are, something that frames and centers reality, something that provides a means to understand what we do not, something that, by in some way constituting, ordering, and presenting existence in a more profound and broader and richer way than we possibly can, sums up, crowns, and defines existence, and enables us to make sense of our lives. Even if we deny the idea of a real and material metaphysical and transcendent, we must nonetheless admit that we cannot make sense of our lives on our own. We cannot see beyond the limits of this world. We need a bigger picture to fully understand our world.

Ironically, although we may believe this, we also realize that we may never fully understand it. Consider this passage from the Hebrew Bible (Ecclesiastes 3:11):

> "God has made all things beautiful in their time. He has also set eternity in their [human] heart, [yet] so that men [and women] will not find out the work which God has done from the beginning even to the end."

What does this mean? Although we have been born with

a longing for and sense of eternity, an intuition of endlessness and ultimate purpose, because we are finite, we will never fully find or know it. We will spend our lives pursuing adventure and exploration and meaning without ever knowing, fully, what everything means or where everything will end up. We know that we can know, but we also know that we will never know fully. Again: the paradox of humanness, the joy and frustration that pervade the life of every human being.[61]

In addition, realize that, ironically, even those of us who are most opposed to the idea of metaphysics do, occasionally, admit to its possibility. Consider this quote from Bertrand Russell, a person who made no secret for his distaste for his distaste for conventional religious conclusions about reality:

> "Even when one feels nearest to other people, something in one seems obstinately to belong to God, and to refuse to enter into any earthly communion--at least that is how I should express it if I thought there was a God. It is odd, isn't it? I care passionately for this world and many things and people in it, and yet . . . what is it all? There must be something more important, one feels, though I don't believe there is."[62]

---

61   See yet another passage from the New Testament, the apostle Paul's first letter to the church at Corinth, that we presently see "through a mirror darkly," unable to see life in full (1 Corinthians 13:12). Also, consider three books recently published on that most enigmatic but singularly profound book of the Hebrew canon, Ecclesiastes, as they are reviewed by J. Gerald Janzen in the May 31, 2011 issue of *the Christian Century*.

62   Excerpted from Bertrand Russell, *Selected Letters of Bertrand Russell: The Public Years, 1914 – 1970* (New York: Routledge, 2002). Compare this with his words about the dangerous futility of religion and

The prospect of metaphysics does not die easily.[63]

Consider as well that a world without transcendence and the metaphysical is a frightfully empty world. It leaves us, as the famous existentialist Jean Paul Sartre aptly pointed out, unbearably lonely, tiny and limited beings in an enormous and overwhelmingly complicated world, devoid of any way to *really* understand the nature of our existence. All we have is ourselves, our lives, and our choices, with no reason as to why we are here, no reason as to why we are the way we are, no reason, really, to be, other than that we are here. And while this may well be enough for many people, it is avoiding the real issue: there is no genuine meaning. Yes, meaning without transcendence is more than possible, but it is a meaning that, ironically, means nothing. Ultimately, it is a meaning that is no meaning at all. So did Sartre opine as he wrote, in the closing lines (before beginning his conclusion) of his *Being and Nothingness,* that, "Man is a useless passion" (or, in the original French, *L'homme est une passion inutile*). More than most people, Sartre realized that if there is no transcendence, no metaphysical, and certainly no God, we and all that we know ultimately mean nothing. We are, to use God's words to Adam in Genesis 3, "dust and to dust [we] shall return" (Genesis 3:19).[64]

---

the metaphysical in *Why I Am Not a Christian* (New York: Simon and Schuster, 1957).

63   In addition, consider the observation that, "human beings almost always seem to have looked to a beyond for the principles of explanations of the sensible world." We naturally and inevitably lean on some form of transcendence for meaning in this immanent experience. See Luc Brisson, *How Philosophers Save Myths* (Chicago: University of Chicago, 2005).

64   Jean Paul Sartre, *Being and Nothingness,* translated by Hazel E. Barnes (New York: Washington Square, 1966). Think, too, about a song by the rock band Kansas, which suggests that ultimately we are nothing

Or as Albert Camus, who, although he was not an existentialist in the manner of Sartre, wrote several novels that greatly informed existentialism, said in his *Myth of Sisyphus,* "I realize that if through science I can seize phenomena and enumerate them, I cannot, for all that, apprehend the world." Even if we can describe the world, Camus is saying, we will never understand it. Life is therefore absurd: why bother even living?[65]

To repeat, transcendence and metaphysics provide the missing link between our perceived and genuinely real physically valid experience and our understanding of it. They establish the final meaning of what is real, presenting for us a framework for examining, analyzing, and describing ultimate meaning. Transcendence and the metaphysical are essential to our well being.

So what does this have to do with the question we posed several pages ago, the question of how can anything just *be?* Unless we assume (and this is a big assumption!) the presence of transcendence and the metaphysical, we will never be able to answer this question. As the laws of thermodynamics rightly observe, our material world cannot simply pop out of nothing. Nothing, to reiterate what we stated earlier, can come out of nothing. In addition, as we noted in our most recent discussion, transcendence and the metaphysical are

---

more than dust in the wind, here today and gone tomorrow, never again to leave a physical mark of our presence (*Dust in the Wind,* written by Kerry Livgren and released on Kirshner Records in 1977).

65   Albert Camus, *The Myth of Sisyphus and Other Essays,* translated by Justin O'Brien (New York: Alfred A. Knopf, 1955). See also Stephen Eric Bonner, *Camus* (Chicago: University of Chicago, 1999). In addition, read Robert Zaretsky, "A Russian Plot? No, a French Obsession" in *New York Times Op-Ed,* August 14, 2011, who notes that Camus insisted that although people believe life to be absurd, they refuse to "accept the possibility of senselessness" which such absurdity inherently implies.

vital to understanding the physical and material. We cannot understand a box unless we can stand outside of it.

Perhaps you think, however, that we are trying to evade the question. If the material cannot just be, how the transcendent and metaphysical just be? Yet as we have noted, unless we posit an uncaused starting point, even if, as we observed repeatedly, we cannot necessarily physically prove its existence, we cannot do without one. Even if we will never know how transcendence and the metaphysical simply "are," we must realize that we need them to make sense of any theory of origins which we may propose. They *must* intrinsically just "be." What else do we have?

Hence, we proceed, as we noted earlier, in the absence of complete proof and logic, but also with the understanding that occasionally we must acknowledge that sometimes our conclusions must necessarily exceed them. From our finite standpoint, we will never understand how anything can just "be," but conversely we will never understand how something could not just "be." Otherwise, nothing means anything.

Let's return to the text. We have already established that in αρχη we see the uncaused cause, the uncaused and beginningless beginning of all things. In αρχη we therefore find one way of viewing what we realize we must have in order to construct a logical and reasonable picture of our origins: a verifiable medium of beginning, a real and, we shall see, testable presence in which all things have their origin. If we are to look at this in terms of our discussion about transcendence and metaphysics, we can say that we see in αρχη a real metaphysical presence, a genuine presence and realm of transcendence.

Yet we do not, at this point, know much about αρχη. If we are to understand αρχη as a meaningful explanation of origins, we need to learn more about it.

Happily, John helps us out. In the αρχη, the beginning,

he writes, was the Word. What's the Word? The English word "Word" is translated from the Greek word λογος. And what does λογος mean? Although the Greeks defined and viewed λογος in a number of ways, we can distill them into two basic ideas. One, λογος was understood as "word" or "speech" (even, in some cases, "event," an idea drawn from the ancient Semitic idea of word (Hebrew "dabhar," Akkadian "dibbah") as activity and effectual presence) something that people use to describe and signify, something they use to symbolize and paint their pictures of the world as they perceive them.

Two, λογος was viewed as a representation of the transcendent and metaphysical, the ethereal and beyond, the unifying order and integration point in which all things find meaning or sensibility (here we see that the Greeks clearly recognized, as did we, that notions of eternity and infinity and transcendence and the metaphysical are essential to developing a proper and reasonable picture of the world). From this standpoint, λογος was almost like God, a sort of ultimate reality or synoptic finality in the universe, the final end point for purpose and meaning in the cosmos.

For this reason, the Greeks also saw the λογος as the ground and fount of what is most worth knowing, the bedrock principle upon which all knowledge and understanding ought to be developed, shaped, and constructed. The λογος is that which gives ideas, thoughts, activities, indeed, all things, meaning. It affirms the essential rationality and meaningfulness of existence.

Or as Slavoj Žižek, employing the insights of Martin Heidegger, put it, the λογος is the "primordial 'gathering' of the senses which opens up a world." It enables existential panorama and global meaning.[66]

To reiterate a point, we might pause here to note, again,

---

66   Slavoj Žižek, *Living in the End Times* (London: Verso, 2011).

that in this conclusion we see that the Greeks implicitly acknowledged that humans cannot understand existence as meaningful without admitting to the existence of a larger framework for doing so. We would agree, and it is not just because, as the writers of the very popular movie *My Big Fat Greek Wedding* claimed, we in the West are all Greeks. We think in these terms because, as we have observed, whether we like it or not, everyone, everyone who is a thinking and feeling human being inevitably harbors an innate propensity to think in terms of ultimacy of form and substance, a natural predilection to ponder things beyond them.[67]

If we put these two broad definitions together, we can conclude that, foremost, the λογος is about communication and meaning. It embodies speech, it defines meaning.[68] This allows us to draw two more conclusions. One, we can say that setting the λογος at the beginning of and prior to all things is to say that words and speech (as we already concluded towards the beginning of this meditation) constitute the bedrock of our existence. Communication lies at the beginning of all things.[69]

We therefore see that over and beyond whatever else he may have intended to do, John affirms one of the most fundamental premises of our humanness. We are communicative beings who live, necessarily, in a communicative world, a world founded in speech and communicative act.

---

67   We refer to the widely successful movie released in the U.S. in 2002 by Gold Circle Films.

68   Or as Emil Brunner sees it, Word is "address," intentional communication with intentional purpose. See Emil Brunner, *The Mediator* (Cambridge: Lutterworth Press, 2002).

69   Or as Plato put it in the *Sophist*, the λογος is verifiable discourse, that is, communication that is sensible and true to what is real. See *Plato's Theory of Knowledge: The Theaetetus and the Sophist,* edited by Francis Cornford (New York: Dover, 2003).

Two, we can say that if the λογος is inherently meaningful and consequently the definer of meaning, and if the λογος was in the beginning, then the beginning of all things is meaningful. This in turn suggests that all things that come out of or follow this beginning are meaningful, too. The universe is therefore innately meaningful. It has purpose.

It is well to note here that we would not be able to draw this conclusion about the universe if we had previously decided that its origins are not embedded in communication and speech, not embedded in specific form and purpose, and that the universe simply emerged, for no apparent reason, from an impersonal nothingness. What would be the point? In adopting John's position, we are saying that we agree that a meaningful presence lies at the origin of the universe. We acknowledge that our origins are inherently and insuperably meaningful.

Moreover, because he finds the universe to be meaningful, John will say that it has value in and of itself. It has a point. And because it has a point, he will go on to observe, the universe has something to be, somewhere to go, a purpose and destiny. It also has something to say. It speaks. The universe communicates; it discloses information about itself, information which, because it stems from a meaningful presence, is intrinsically meaningful, too. Bottom line, as John sees it, the universe is revelation, an intrinsically revelatory experience. It communicates, it discloses, it unfolds, it promises. The universe is a wide open experience of meaningful possibilities and eventualities.

In his presentation of the λογος, John therefore confirms nearly every one of the conclusions we drew earlier, namely, that one, the universe is meaningful; two, the universe speaks; and three, the universe is a communicative experience. And why is this? The universe is meaningful and a communicative experience because it is grounded in and stems from a meaningful and communicative presence. Something bigger than the universe, that is, the λογος, an innately communicative presence that preceded the universe, ensured that it would be this way. The universe is not communicative by accident; something intended for it to be this way. Something intended for the universe to have communicative capacities, something intended for the universe to have value, purpose, something intended for it to have a point. The universe is not random. There is a reason why it is here, there is a reason why it communicates, there is a reason why it is meaningful. The λογος guarantees the legitimacy and presence of a meaningful universe, one that is populated, as the lives of every animal species, including our own demonstrate, by meaningful beings who have meaningful experiences. Existence means more than living.

Put another way, we can say that the λογος embodies that which is most important to the integrity of the human experience in this world. In all the universe, nothing is more essential to philosophical totality and existential meaning than the λογος. The λογος is the beginning of what is possible and meaningful in existence. Without the λογος, without the inherent meaningfulness it implants in the universe (and everything, including you and me, in it), the universe really has no meaning (recall Sartre's words about people being "useless passions").

Consider this: although we may have experiences that we find meaningful, we only believe them to be meaningful because we say they are. We have no independent way to verify our assertions. We are only congratulating ourselves for ourselves![70]

Furthermore, we can tell ourselves anything and believe it to be meaningful, but this does not mean that it is. We need

---

70 When we use the term existential, we refer to the experience of existence, that is, the existential experience is simply the experience of being alive on this planet.

to know something is meaningful not because we *think* that it is, but because evidence and information which we did not invent or create (but which we find in our lives) tells us that it is. For us to constitute genuine meaning, we need to know that the world is grounded in meaningfulness, a meaningfulness that we did not make or create (for if we think we had, we would be back to square one: how would we know it?). It is this meaningfulness that ensures that, when we seek and enjoy meaning, we are actually doing so, that we are actually participating in meaningful forms and structures and not shooting into the dark, claiming to have meaning in what, if it does not have a personal origin, may well be a meaningless universe. It is this meaningfulness that establishes the meaningfulness of our lives. It is this meaningfulness, an antecedent and holistic meaningfulness, that guarantees meaningfulness in our present and existential experience.

And we have this meaning before us: the λογος.

We cannot underestimate the revolutionary nature of this conclusion. Richard Dawkins, one of the twentieth-first century's most outspoken (and famous) atheists, was once asked about the meaning of life. "This is not a legitimate question," he replied. Dawkins displays an acute grasp of the stakes at hand. Unless something bigger and more meaningful than we, be it the λογος or something else, affirms the fact and presence of meaning in the universe, we indeed have no reason to ask about life's meaning: there is none! Apart from an idea like the λογος, the world as we experience it has absolutely no meaning. There is no reason why it is here and, clearly, no reason why we are here, either. To recall Sartre's words once more, we are simply "useless passions." Indeed: as Sartre and Dawkins so ably articulate, apart from a meaningful beginning, we are pointless.[71]

---

71   As quoted in Jesse Bering's *Belief Instinct: the Psychology of Souls, Destiny, and the Meaning of Life* (New York: W. W. Norton, 2011).

However, apart from us obtaining any other information about the λογος, we are, in a way, too. Even if we say that the λογος enables or ensures meaning, we still do not know how it does so. We still do not know how we can find this meaning. Unless we know more about the λογος, though we may *think* that we are meaningful, we still do not know *why* we are meaningful. And if we do not know why we are meaningful, we have accomplished nothing, really. We are still left with having to tell ourselves we are meaningful without any legitimate reason, other than our assumed and asserted existence of a physically unprovable λογος, to do so. We must learn more about the λογος.

Before we do, let's take some moments to talk further about the importance of an idea we mentioned some time ago, the idea of revelation. In its most basic sense, revelation refers to the communication, in a variety of forms, of information which had not been previously known. It is the disclosure of information which had not been known previously, information which, despite all human attempts to acquire exhaustive knowledge of the world, has, to this point, been unknown.

Revelation comes in a nearly infinite array of forms. It ranges from information we share about ourselves to another, information that a teacher communicates to her students, information that a leader shares with her nation, and on and on. In every instance, however, revelation is the unveiling and consequent perception, in some way, of information that had heretofore been unknown to the party who is receiving it.

This is why we claimed that world is a revelatory experience. Every moment of every day, it discloses new information about itself, information which we did not previously know. The world's speech, in all its varieties and forms, is revelation. This includes the physical phenomena we see, phenomena such as mountains, oceans, and animals, things that, even for a moment, may stir our hearts and souls, things that cause us to develop new ideas about who we are and to think anew about what life means. Yet it also includes emotions and feeling, the emotions and feelings that we experience in the course of living our lives, emotions like hope, faith, and love, emotions that open up new doorways and paths in our hearts and lives, emotions that unfold new ideas about who we are. Revelation can be intellectual, too, insights that we gain in the course of examining a particular facet of the human adventure, or conclusions to which we come as we study the vast base of knowledge which people have built up over the many millennia they have filled the earth. It's all the world's revelation, it's all what we learn from living on this globe. In every way, as we live, as we live and breathe and engage in life, we experience the revelation that is the world as we know it. To live is to experience the revelation of the raw and incomprehensible fact of existence, the continuing marvel of being alive on this planet, every moment of every day.

As we continue to work through the text before us, however, we must think about revelation in more than this way. We must think about revelation as information which is communicated to us, we earthly beings, from the metaphysical and transcendent. We must view revelation as the intentional disclosure of information about realms of whose essence we do not precisely know, information that comes from intelligent presences which occupy those realms as an ongoing fact of their lives and being. If we agree that we need a real and physical (in some sense) transcendent and metaphysical to make sense of our world, this view of revelation makes perfect sense. We see revelation as information which we need to develop a full and proper perspective on our lives and the universe in which we live them. We see revelation as the essential disclosure of the metaphysical and transcendent to us, disclosure which we require to live a meaningful existence.

As the writer of Proverbs 29 (from the Hebrew Bible) observes, without revelation, that is, without information about the transcendent and metaphysical, we have no real guidelines as to how we will live or understand our world. As one translation puts it, we "perish," not in a physical sense, but in a spiritual one. We are left without data or verifiable insight about ultimate and transcending meaning. Life is hopeless.[72]

We say all this because this is the direction that John is going in our text. He has already indicated that our beginnings are set into an eternal and uncaused cause, an αρχη that, in some unfathomable way, has always been, has always existed. Moreover, he has told us that amidst and in this αρχη exists something he calls the λογος, an idea which his audience is accustomed to using to make sense of the world. But now we shall see that John will claim that, in addition to all these things, because the λογος is the source of meaning and because the λογος was in the beginning, the λογος reveals essential and true information about the metaphysical and transcendent, the fundamental starting points, as we have observed, of all being. The λογος is revelation, revelation in its fullest and most important sense, revelation that will reveal not only the sensible and physical, but revelation that will unfold the meaning of the formational underpinnings of our universe. The λογος speaks. And it speaks about things that we would not learn on our own, things of the metaphysical and transcendent, things that are absolutely crucial to us fully grasping the nature of reality.

At this point, John turns an important corner, one that leads him to a view of the λογος radically different from that of most of his audience. He will claim that not only is the λογος revelation, it is personal revelation as well, personal revelation

---

72   This translation is from the King James version of the Bible, first published in 1611.

that is deliberately disclosed by a personal being. The λογος is therefore not like the impersonal speech of the impersonal world, the speech of the rivers and sky and deserts (although as many people will attest, these natural phenomena speak, often profoundly, to us, and together constitute very powerful enablers of existential understanding). The λογος is personal revelation, revelation that is given with personal intent and personal purpose. It is revelation of a someone, a personal someone, and not an insensate something. It is personal revelation from and about a personal and meaningful and purposeful metaphysical and transcendent.[73]

As we already stated, however, the Greeks in no way saw the λογος as personal. For them, the λογος was not someone to whom they might look or pray for advice, help, or guidance. It was simply there, a good and necessary idea, but one without genuine physical substance, something that helps render things sensible yet something that had no material form or substance, something with no actual physical basis in reality. It had no personal relationship with the creation because it did not really exist. It was an idea and nothing more. The λογος was the impersonal and formless Aristotelian unmoved mover, the ultimate activator and center of meaning that, ironically, had no inner form in itself. And it certainly could not be known. Moreover, as an idea and nothing more than an idea, its existence could not be definitively proven. To do so would be impossible.[74]

---

73 Native American religion testifies amply to the legitimacy of the natural world as a venue for finding meaning. See, for just a few examples among many, A. L. Kroeber, *Handbook of the Indians of California* (New York: Dover, 1976), Sylvanus G. Morley, *The Ancient Maya,* third edition (Stanford: Stanford University, 1956), Peter Thompkins, *Mysteries of the Mexican Pyramids* (New York: Harper & Row, 1976), and James R. Walker's *Lakota Belief and Ritual,* cited previously.

74 On the "unmoved mover" in Aristotle, see Book 12 of his *Metaphysics,* translated by W. D. Ross, in *The Complete Works, op cit.*

John understands very well that this will not do. After all, what good is a mute and impersonal meaningfulness? Yes, personal beings can find meaning in impersonal things, but eventually they will want to find meaning in personal things, things to which they can most directly and effectually relate. Although we may think that an impersonal λογος may have made the universe meaningful, though we may think that it may have made *us* meaningful, we ultimately delude ourselves if we suppose that it really did so. How do we really know? Moreover, as we noted earlier, how can something that is essentially impersonal create something that is personal? And how could it communicate with a personal being? It could not. Forever and ever, it will remain beyond it, always remote and ultimately inaccessible to it.

If we are to look at this from another angle, we might say that if the λογος is personal and is the source of communicability, purpose, and meaning and yet is not able to communicate with that which it has endowed with personality and meaning, how can it ever be, from our standpoint, anything *other* than this unknown beginning? How can it ever be anything other than an inscrutable and ethereal yet necessary starting point to existence? If this were the extent of the λογος in our experience, we would never know the λογος as it is. We would never know, would never *really* know that which gives us and our reality meaning.

The λογος's metaphysicality compounds the problem. By virtue of what it is, the λογος must *be* "beyond" our existence. It must not be exactly like you and me. If it were like us, the λογος would in no way be capable of generating a universe! Yet if the λογος exists "beyond" existence, resident in the realm of transcendence and the metaphysical, and therefore very much unlike us, how would we start to get to know it? We cannot know the infinite, we cannot know the eternal: what are we therefore to do? The λογος remains forever beyond us.

How can we know the source of what gives our life meaning?

Let's keep reading. "And the λογος [from this point we will call the λογος, "Word"] was with God," John continues, "and the Word was God." (For context, refer to the full passage as it is quoted above.)

These are weighty words. On the one hand, they solve the problem. They tell us who Word (λογος) is. Word is God.

On the other hand, they raise another problem. Who or what is God? Although people have many, many ways of defining God, most of us agree that, whatever else he/she/it may be, God is significant. God is someone/something bigger and greater than we, someone/something that in some way gives, with various levels of finality, form, definition, and meaning to our lives and reality. Whether God is an idea, a person, a presence, or something else altogether, most of us who believe in God or at least the idea of him/her/it will agree that God is someone/something special and significant.[75]

Nonetheless, as we observed, God has many different meanings to people. Calling Word God does not therefore so much necessarily define Word with specificity as it defines Word as "someone" or "something" in our experience. As we saw how the words that Adam used to name the animals made them real to him, so calling Word God makes Word real to us. It makes Word more than an amorphous and distant and unfathomable infinite and uncaused beginning, more than formless originative plasma. It gives presence and form to Word, gives shape and definition to a thought, an idea that, as

---

75   Of course, as any Greek in John's audience knew, because the Greeks defined the gods in human images, though these gods may have been physically larger and more powerful than their human counterparts, they were in no way *morally* greater than their human counterparts!

a personal actuality, was previously unknown to us. Calling Word God unfolds Word as an object of our perception, a tangible point in our world. It gives Word working visibility, on some level, in our experience. We can get to know Word, can get to know, after a fashion, Word as a person, a person to whom we finite human beings may be able to, eventually, directly relate, a person whom we call God. We see Word in a personally experiential way, an immediate and personal point of significance and meaning in our lives.

Most significantly, identifying Word as God means that we are identifying Word as revelation (indeed, as we shall see, *the* revelation) about God. Word is the revelation of the metaphysical and transcendent, palpable and tangible information about the supernatural that lies beyond us.

In concluding this, we also understand that if, as we observed, Word is eternal, present as well as presence in the uncaused beginning, God must be eternal and present and presence in the uncaused beginning, too. Also, God must be personal. How important is this? If we conclude that God is an "it," that is, that he is no more than a massive glob of plasma, we may as well stop right here, as we are back to the familiar dilemma, one which we have cited many times, of trying to find the possibility of a personal creation in the unconscious and voiceless rumblings of impersonal substance. Clearly, a "something" has no personality, much less eternality (how it would acquire either one?). Hence, if we wish to experience God (or, as John noted, Word) genuinely and personally meaningful, we must decide to understand God a personal and eternally living being. As we observed in our previous mention of *If You're Afraid of the Dark, Remember the Night Rainbow,* it is hard to feel genuine oneness with a rock. If God is to be anything to us, God must be a personal being. And if God is to be of any real value to us, God must be an eternal being. If God dies just as we do, of what real use is he?

We do not need a mortal god to remind ourselves of what we already know.[76]

If God is indeed personal, and if Word is God, we conclude that Word is personal, too. Moreover, as Word has indeed "been" in the uncaused beginning, always and forever existing, we can therefore say that Word is an eternally existing *personal* being as well. As God, Word is a personal being who was not born, nor as God, will Word as a personal being ever die. As God, Word always was, always is, and always will be. Word is eternal, and Word is eternally personal. Word is the eternal and always living God, patently transcendent and imminently metaphysical, the ultimate and uncaused being. As God is forever, so is Word.

For John's Jewish readers, these words should have been no surprise. They had always believed that God is eternal. For instance, every one of them was familiar with God's response to Moses' query, as it is recorded in the Book of Exodus, about whom he should say is sending him to liberate the Hebrews from their slavery in Egypt. "I am that I am," God replied, reminding Moses that he was the one who has always been, the one who has always been living, and the one who always will continue to be living. I, God was saying to Moses, am eternal.[77]

For John's Greek readers, however, it was another story. Maybe it is yours, too: how can anything, much less God and his word, be eternal? How can God, whoever he is, be

---

76   As the Hebrew Bible as well as the New Testament uniformly render God as a "he" (while understanding that God ultimately transcends such things, at least as we humans understand them, and that he is in truth "spirit" (John 4:24)), we will do the same. For a dissenting view, see the many books by the late Mary Daly, including *Beyond God the Father: Toward a Philosophy of Women's Liberation* (Boston: Beacon Press, 1993).

77   See the account in Exodus 3:1-14. The phrase on which we are focusing is based on the participial form of *hayah,* the word for "be."

a personal and eternally living being? As we have noted earlier, however, it is exceedingly difficult, if not impossible, to conceive of origins without the fact of infinity and the notion of eternity. In addition, it is equally difficult to explain the presence of personality in the universe without positing the presence of an eternally originative personality. If God is to be God as most of us would like to envision him, he must be personal, and he must be eternal.

John knew that he needed to begin to give definition to Word. He knew that if he did not, Word would forever remain, as we noted earlier, a necessary but unreachable "everything," a critical ingredient in affirming the integrity of reality, but one which is personally untouchable in our lives. The bedrock meaningfulness of our meaningful and communicative existence would remain forever unknown. We, perhaps the most personal of all personal beings, would be alone in an apparently (for we would have no way to definitively prove otherwise) impersonal universe. God would still be gone.

Let's back up a bit. As we noted, before the text says that the Word is God, it states that the Word was with God. What does this mean? How can something be *with* someone else and yet also *be* that someone else? It's a vexing question.

To answer this question properly, let us first remind ourselves that, contrary to the way the Greeks viewed the λογος, Word, as John saw it, is personal, entirely and profoundly personal. Word is constituted to inevitably and invariably interact with other personal beings and the world in which they live, and to do so in thoroughly personal ways. Word exists to engage in communal exchange, to freely enter into communicative interplay with personal beings. It is the nature of Word to participate in personal interaction and exchange.

As it is for God. If Word is personal, and if Word is God, God is personal. Like Word, like you and me, God is one who is constituted to engage in personal communion and exchange. God's nature, God's bent is to interact in personal ways with personal beings.

With whom do Word and God engage? Word and God engage with each other. Always and forever, Word and God have communed and communicated with each other, and always and forever, Word and God have related to and connected with each other as personal beings. From all eternity, Word and God have been communicating together.

But this does not fully answer our question. How can Word exist at the beginning with God, yet be God, too? Does God exist with himself? On the one hand, sure: we all exist with ourselves. We all know ourselves. We all talk to ourselves. Unless we are total hermits, however, we all exist with other people, too.[78] We talk with other people, we work with other people, we live with other people. That is, in part, how we know we are personal, and that is, in part, how we know we are communicative. We find ourselves in each other.[79]

On the other hand, however, we exist with ourselves as only one being: ourselves. But the text seems to say that Word exists with God, but that he is God as well. Put another way,

---

78 For instance, consider the Hindu mystics of whom Anita Desai writes in her many novels about the Indian culture, the mystics who live alone in remote jungles and who have supposedly not slept in twenty-five years. Even they began as interactive beings. See her *Journey to Ithaca* (New York: Penguin, 1996).

79 There is one caveat to this, however: although postmodernity avers that we constitute ourselves in being with each other, it remains clear that we are and construct ourselves apart from other people. We find our selves in community, yet, but we also have a distinctive identity, a distinctive self. We had not lost our "self." On this, see, among many others, Charles Taylor's *Secular Age* (Cambridge: Harvard University, 2007).

Word exists as two beings, God and Word. How can this be?

Let's think about what we do know. We know that for all eternity God and Word, both personal beings, have been in communion and exchange with each other. We also know that although if God is to be God, he doesn't need anyone else to tell him that he is personal and communicative—he intrinsically knows this about himself—God really only expresses the fact of his personhood when he interacts with another personal being. We might say that God needs Word to be fully personal, not in essence, but in practice, and Word needs God to be the same in turn. Moreover, if Word is not God, John's entire argument collapses. Why would anyone place her faith in a material and finite beginning? Yet if Word is God, how can Word be an independent and self-sustaining being, a being whom we might want to know? It doesn't seem to make sense.

Yet consider this: forever and ever, God and Word have been in communion with each other. Forever and ever, God and Word have, one, been aware that they are whom they are; two, been aware that they are beings who are aware that they are aware of whom they are; and three, been aware that they are beings who are aware they communicate with other beings. Forever and ever, God and Word have known themselves as personal beings.

Again, God and Word know themselves as personal beings not only because they intrinsically understand themselves as such as a fundamental part of their nature, but because for all eternity they have been experiencing it in their exchanges with each other. God and Word communicate with each other—and know that they are doing so—yet they are both in the uncaused beginning as distinctive beings. They cannot be otherwise. God and Word have always been as they are, have always been as they are together, separate and distinctive beings yet always together as personal beings, sharing the same personal essence and beingness.

On the other hand, if we follow this thesis further, we bump into one of the thorniest problems in biblical theology. How can God exist as more than one person? Rather than work ourselves into knots which we will never fully untangle trying to answer this question, let us just say for now that, based on a comprehensive reading of the Bible, this seems to be the only reasonable conclusion to draw about the nature of God. The Bible clearly identifies three beings as equally God—the Father, the Son, and the Holy Spirit (a divine being who appears in the Hebrew Bible as the "Spirit of God" and in the Dead Sea Scrolls, written a couple of hundred years after the completion of the Old Testament canon, as "Holy Spirit"[80])—yet the Bible also holds that these three beings nonetheless comprise and present and express one God. They share, participate in, and express the divine nature, substance, and essence in equal measure and relation, yet they are distinct persons as they do so. Theologians call this the Trinity: three beings in one, yet three distinct beings nonetheless.[81]

This is the only way that we can understand John's assertion. Word is God, yet Word is also with God: one God, two persons, two equal persons who are in equal and perpetual communion with each other. (Again, although the third person of the Trinity, the Holy Spirit, is fully divine and

---

80   On the Dead Sea Scrolls, one of the most sensational archaeological discoveries of the last century, see *The Complete Dead Sea Scrolls in English*, translated by Geza Vermes (New York: Penguin, 1997).

81   If you still find yourself flummoxed by this conclusion, I recommend you consult any of several good books on Christian theology, particularly the recently published *The Christian Faith* by Michael Horton (Grand Rapids: Zondervan, 2011). See also Thomas C. Oden's *The Living God* (Peabody, Massachusetts: Prince, 1992, 2001).

equally important to the essence, definition, and concept of the Godhead, a full and proper discussion of him lies outside the scope of this book.[82])

Given John's background, his words should not startle us. As a good Jew, John knew the creation account in Genesis very well. Although the opening lines of this account present God, and God alone, creating the heavens and earth, it describes God differently when it announces the creation of humanity. It uses a plural noun to identify God, recording God as saying, "Let *us* make" humanity "in *our* image, according to *our* likeness" (see Genesis 1:26). These words, coming at the very beginning of the Bible, suggest that, even in one of the oldest sections of Scripture, the Hebrews (who, through various historical and linguistic circumstance, eventually came to be known as Jews) already had an inkling that the being of God is perhaps expressed in more than one person.

In addition, John knew, as did his Jewish readers, about Proverbs 8. In highly poetic language, Proverbs 8 presents wisdom (one of the most treasured concepts of Judaism) as a woman, a woman who is calling and summoning all humanity to come to her, for, she claims, she is the best path, the most right way for people to pursue. Wisdom is a patently personal and purifying experience.[83]

Wisdom is eternal, too. Before the creator brought the creation into existence, the proverb tells us, wisdom was there, right at his side. Like Word was with God, wisdom was with the creator, right from the very beginning, indeed, even before the beginning (Hebrew *rosh*). Wisdom was with God, the text notes, before anything else came to be. Wisdom

---

82   Again, see the references I mention in the preceding footnote.

83   In addition to its elevation in Proverbs 8, wisdom is lauded in Kabbalah, a profound expression of Jewish mysticism. On this, see Daniel C. Matt, *The Essential Kabbalah* (New Jersey: Castle Books, 1997).

and the creator were and are in eternal dialogue with the other.[84]

Hence, although John was well aware of the Torah's assertion (Deuteronomy 6:4) that, "the Lord God is one," he realized that in Word he saw the living personification of the word of God as it appears in Genesis 1:3, the word which spoke light into existence. He also saw in Word the living expression of Proverbs 8's eternal wisdom, the eternal wisdom that, with God, had created the world. In addition, he saw in Word the earthly form of the resurrecting spirit of life as it is presented in Ezekiel 37, the spirit that gives new life to a valley of dry bones. John could therefore not deny that the fact of Word being with God, while being God as well, totally transformed Deuteronomy's assertion of divine essence. Although he believed the Lord God to be "one," in presenting the notion of Word as God, John was indicating that he also believed that the one Lord God expressed himself in more than one way. God exists as one, he concluded, yet comes to us in plurality, a plural experience, an experience of three persons who, though they are three distinct personalities, nonetheless share and express exactly the same divine nature and essence.[85]

Hence, even if we have trouble accepting the idea of the Trinity, we must realize that it is deeply embedded in the

---

84   As the prophet Jeremiah, writing in the sixth and seventh centuries B.C., notes, "It is He [God] who made the earth by His power, who established the world by His wisdom, and by His understanding He stretched out the heavens" (Jeremiah 51:15).

85   In regard to Deuteronomy 6:4, which states that the Lord God is one, consider the reaction of the high priest Caiaphas when Jesus, quoting a passage from the prophet Daniel, informed him that he was the Son of Man, a fully divine being who would come in the clouds of heaven to render justice on the earth: this, Caiaphas declared, was blasphemy! He could not yet fully accept the idea of a Trinity (Mark 14:53-65).

Bible and the community which, over a period of roughly fifteen hundred years, wrote it, and if we therefore wish to understand how to apply our thinking about Word to our world today, we must acknowledge its existence. As we have previously admitted to the necessity of an uncaused beginning as the working (and not fully understandable) paradox which provides the only reasonable explanation for origins, so we accept the necessity of the idea of the Trinity, again, even if we do not fully understand it, as a necessary explanatory paradox for completing a sensible and reasonable, though still partly unfathomable picture of God.[86]

Regardless of where we land on this issue, however, the central point is that because Word is personal, it is inherently intentional and fully aware that it creates and illuminates (see John 1:4-5 as they are presented above). It is fully aware that it has given the universe meaning, highly cognizant that it has given this unspeakably massive and rapidly expanding cosmos its beginning, form, essence, and point. It is also aware that it has a reason for doing this, aware that it birthed and enlightened this cosmos with specificity, value, and purpose.

Moreover, as we noted above, Word knows that it is self-aware. Consider a dog. Is a dog aware of itself? Yes, the dog is aware of itself, but as to whether a dog knows that it is a dog, we must say no. The dog has no transcending and detached

---

86 In truth, when we speak of origins, we are talking inherently about mystery, for clearly, no one (no human being, anyway) was around to see how the universe really began. To a certain extent, any way we choose to go, we go by faith. And we base this faith on the evidence that this event of origins left behind, the living evidence of ourselves and our world. Hence, because we understand that we are personal beings who live in a communicative and revelatory world, we choose to understand our origins in personal terms, the personal presence of a personal and eternally living divine being: God. It is the evidence of whom we are that drives us to this conclusion. Again, the impersonal simply cannot create the personal.

way of looking at or describing itself and its world. It simply exists, unaware that it is a dog, though entirely aware, in its own way, that it is nonetheless here.

But the dog doesn't know what being here means. Or to paraphrase the philosopher Martin Heidegger, it doesn't know what it is to "dasein", to be "there" in the world.[87]

Word is therefore not only self-aware, it knows that it is as such. It is the cognizant uncaused beginning, very much aware that it is the self-aware uncaused beginning from which everything else has come.

We might pause here and note that, in seemingly every way, Word is like us. Word is personal, Word communicates, Word exists with other persons, and Word creates and moves and acts. Yet Word remains two things we are not: infinite and eternal, points of difference whose significance we shall see more clearly later (if we do not already!).

Let's continue. As we noted earlier, as John would have it, the Word is effectively a cause without a cause, a (in fact, the only possible) uncaused cause of the universe. It is a cause without a beginning, a cause that is eternal and infinite, a cause that is outside of temporal and spatial constraints and that is not controlled by anything other than itself. It is totally self-existent and self-empowering. Word exists, but it is also beyond existence, at least as you and I see it, for it is eternal. Similarly, although Word is "there," it is also bigger than "there," for it is infinite, unbound by any notion of "there." It is everywhere, all at once. If Word could see (and we shall eventually see that it can), it would see a movie all at once.

Also, as we observed, according to John, Word is none other than that most mysterious yet seemingly necessary, in

---

87   For more information than you may want to know about *Dasein,* see Heidegger's *Being and Time,* translated by Joan Stambaugh (Albany: State University of New York, 1996).

some way, of beings, God. Word is not impersonal matter or substance, but a definable personal object. Word is God.

As God, for what is Word responsible? According to John, Word is responsible for nothing less than the creation of the universe. Through Word (see verse 1:3 as we presented it above), John observes, "all things came into being" and apart from Word, "nothing came into being that has not come into being."

The text is very clear on this point. The Greek word used here, παντα (all), denotes comprehensive coverage of all possibilities. There really is nothing that Word, as God, did not bring into being. Nothing exists besides what Word (God) purposed and intended should exist.[88]

More importantly, however, if we are to connect John's account with the creation account in Genesis 1 (which, as I hope you have already seen, is more than possible to do: the Bible is a highly coherent and connected book), we see that Word (God) created all things by simply, as it were, *speaking* them into existence. Speech created the world, speech shaped and molded the world. Speech is the creator and foundation of the universe. The world was created through speech.[89]

(And it did so, as the medieval Christian mystic Thomas á Kempis notes in his *Meditations, with Prayers, on the Life and Loving-Kindness of our Lord and Saviour Jesus Christ*, "without any labour." Word (God) is the ultimate and unaided power of genesis and being.[90])

---

88 Or as the beautiful and ancient Gaelic hymn *Morning has Broken* puts it, "praise for them ["singing" and "the morning"] springing fresh from the Word."

89 See Genesis 1:3, "Then God said, 'Let there be light,' and there was light." God created with nothing more (and nothing less) than his speech.

90 Thomas á Kempis, *Meditations, with Prayers, on the Life and Loving-Kindnesses of our Lord and Saviour, Jesus Christ* (London: E. Dilly, 1760). Kempis also wrote the much better known *Imitation of Christ*.

And if speech connotes meaning, as we observed it does, we see clearly that by "speaking" the universe into existence, Word affirms the meaningfulness of every created thing. Word's speech, the speech that birthed life and reality, weaves meaning into every corner of the cosmos. Hence, whatever else we may conclude about ourselves or our existence, we realize that, again, over and above all else, we are meaningful. We have a reason to be.

And so does the universe.

Once more, John earns his keep. He has already given us a way to understand why we and our world are communicative and meaningful. Now he gives us a definitive explanation for why we and our fellow animals are personal beings. To repeat, because Word is the source of life, and because Word is personal, we ourselves are personal. We are the personal creations of a personal creator.

What does this mean? Recall the words of Richard Dawkins that we considered a few pages earlier. Like any evolutionist, Mr. Dawkins would like to think that this universe emerged from wholly impersonal matter which over billions and billions of years came to somehow exude and develop beings with personality and moral sensibility. Although based on some of the physical evidence we have for cosmological origins this may seem to make sense, in many other ways it does not. Are we really to believe that personal beings evolved and emerged out of blank and impersonal matter? Are we really to believe that cosmic dust, over billions and billions of years, produced human beings? Can chemical interaction and exchange really generate personality? It's exceedingly difficult to see how. Moreover, even if we grant Dawkins this point (although I do not think we need to), we are left with the even more challenging task of proving how chemicals and plasma developed a moral sensibility. How can chemicals produce a sense of right and wrong? The idea strains credulity. Yes, evolution can explain why people might have wanted to be good (for example, that people realized that doing good proved to be a more effective way to preserve the species), but it does not explain *why* people wanted to be good or bad in the first place. It can only explain the uses to which humans put this apparently innate sense of moral conscience in the course of their historical adventures.[91]

It is difficult to deny that personality must have a personal origin. Again: do mountains physically give birth to the animals that inhabit them? No: they simply provide an environment out of which they come and in which they can live.

Once again, John provides good support for another of our previous conclusions, that because it is a personal experience for personal beings, the spoken and created speech of a personal God, the universe speaks. It is designed to reveal and communicate. And the universe communicates because it has been spoken, that is, "worded" and "speeched" into existence. It is the personal creation of a personal being, the intentional construction of an intentional mind. The universe speaks because it is the product of a communicative and therefore purposeful being.

---

91 On this point, see, among many, James Q. Wilson's *The Moral Sense* (New York: Free Press, 1993), which asserts that the moral sense is perhaps a product of culture as much as anything and therefore easily explainable, as well as Dawkins's books (*The Ancestors Tale: A Pilgrimage to the Dawn of Evolution* (New York: Houghton Mifflin, 2004) and *A Devil's Chaplin: Reflections on Hope, Science, Lies, and Love* (New York: Houghton Mifflin, 2003), Jerry Coyne's *Why Evolution is True* (New York: Penguin, 2010), and the books of Stephen Jay Gould, including *The Structure of Evolutionary Theory* (Cambridge: Harvard University, 2002) and *Dinosaur in a Haystack: Reflections in Natural History* (New York: Harmony, 1995). To all these books, however, we must say that, try as they might, they still cannot answer this most important of questions: why are humans moral? For more, see, among many others, C. S. Lewis, *Mere Christianity* (San Francisco: Harper, 2001).

(Granted a speaking being could create something that does not speak, but this does not mean that this speaking being will *always* create something without speech. The point is that this speaking being is capable of creating a speaking being. And if a speaking being creates a personal being, that being will, in some way, speak. Do not most babies learn to speak?[92])

Of course, when John notes that Word has created all things and that nothing that has life or existence has them without Word, he is simply reaffirming and extending ancient Hebrew understandings of the relationship between God and the universe. Yet he is also confirming for us, as he has been doing all along, what we have previously realized is the only way that we can legitimately view ourselves and our world. He is underscoring that, as we have observed, we and the world are inherently personal, the personal and meaningful creations of a personal and meaningful God. The further we dig into John's gospel, it seems, the more we see that what he is saying affirms precisely what we have concluded seems to be the most reasonable and logical way to think about ourselves and the reality in which we live our lives.

Put another way, John is reminding his audience that God (Word) is the beginning of all things, that God, in the person of Word, has brought all things to life, and that furthermore God, in the person of Word, has granted light, the light of what we may preliminarily call wisdom (think about our brief look at Proverbs 8 above) and life, to his creation. Through his speech, God as Word made the creation. And as Word,

---

92   Sadly, due to various congenital deformities, some babies never do grow up to speak. See Janet Morel, *A Theology of Disability and the Church*, which appeared in the Spring 2011 issue of *Fuller Focus*, a publication of Fuller Theological Seminary, located in Pasadena, California. See as well Thomas Reynolds, *Vulnerable Communion: A Theology of Disability and Hospitality* (Grand Rapids: Brazos, 2008).

God spoke: he communicated the universe into existence and endowed it with abiding purpose. Although John is writing in a different language and occupying a different milieu than the writer of Genesis, his thought is the same. A personal God created a personal universe.

In addition, we should note that John is affirming for us what we concluded at the outset of this meditation: speech and communication lie at the heart of the creation. Communication is the beginning of reality and meaning. Communication and personality define and describe the heart of the universe.

And Word is the genesis of it all.

Where does this leave us? We can draw several conclusions. One, the universe is here for a reason. It is not here by accident, nor is it here by whim or impersonal fate. It is here because someone, a personal being, namely, God, Word, the λογος, personally and directly wanted it to be here. The universe is here not because it wanted to be here, but because someone else wanted it to be here. In other words, the universe did not decide to bring itself into existence, nor did it make itself, on its own, on its own power, come to be. To the universe, its existence is unexpected and involuntary. It didn't plan to be here. But someone else intended for it to be so.

And here it is.

Two, as a personal universe, the universe is a grounding, a foundation and medium for personal beings. It is possible to be a personal being in this personal universe. It is possible to experience personal exchange and growth in this cosmos. Most significantly, it is possible to engage in communication, to enter into meaningful interaction with other personal beings and, in a sense, with impersonal entities as well. Creatures with communicative capacities can, if they choose to do so, communicate, with themselves, the world, and God.

Three, a personal universe, as the psalmist noted (see the opening lines of Psalm 19[93]), is a universe that communicates. It speaks. As a result, the personal beings in this universe can experience it, can see and hear it, and can come, in various modes and ways, to understand it.

Four, a personal universe is a meaningful universe. Created by a personal creator, it is here for a reason. It has meaning, it has a point. The universe has meaning in what it is, but it also has meaning because that which birthed it granted it, by dint of its innate creative activity and power, a meaning that defines it (the meaning of its meaning). A progeny of purpose and agency, the universe has inherent and transcendent meaning, a meaning that will be present even if those within it do not always see or experience it. Even if we do not find meaning in ourselves or the universe, we and the universe nevertheless have meaning. And we are meaningful because something bigger than us has, by purposely bringing us and our world into existence, made us so. This means that even if, for whatever reason, we do not acknowledge the existence of personal transcendent meaning in this reality, we will nonetheless find a measure of meaning in it. We live in a universe which a transcendent God designed and made to be intrinsically meaningful. Meaning is available, and it is available to everyone, regardless of what she may believe.

And it all begins with Word.

Let's look at this from another angle. We have claimed, on the basis of John's text, that something we call Word (the λογος) has always been, that it had no beginning, but rather always was, self-existing and needing nothing. Before anything else was or came to be, Word experienced existence, self-empowerment,

---

93   As Psalm 19:1 tells us, "The heavens are telling of the glory of God, and their expanse is declaring the work of his hands." Consider also the famous oratorio by Hayden of the same name.

and autonomy, freely and without limit, deliberation, or restraint. We assert this because we realize that, all things being equal (*mutatis mutandis*), and despite the obvious intellectual challenges it presents, we are on firmer ground to suppose that a personal "someone" rather than an impersonal "something" preceded and wrought the created order. We understand that this is the best way to explain how personality and meaning permeate our existential experience. An impersonal and mute creator could not create a personal and talking universe.[94]

And it certainly could not ensure meaning. On the other hand, as the λογος, the final integrating point and unifying principle, Word is also the verifier, definer, and centering point of all things. Word, that is, communication and speech, is the absolute and ultimate epistemological reference for the universe and any meaning that may be present in it. Word is the working glue that holds the cosmos together. If Word created and gave life to all things, Word also gives meaning to all things. Does not an artist give meaning to whatever she creates?[95]

Also, we can say that in Word is the path to knowing why we are the way we are. As the originator of communication and the instiller and purveyor of meaning, Word enables us to affirm why we are meaningful, why we have an inherent spirit of inquiry and wonder in our lives, and why we seem born to seek and explore and examine our lives and experience.

---

94 For more on the integrity and reliability of the Bible, see, to name just a few, F. F. Bruce, *The New Testament Documents: Are They Reliable?* (Grand Rapids: William B. Eerdmans, 1981), Ben Witherington III, *The New Testament Story* (Grand Rapids: William B. Eerdmans, 2004), and William Lane Craig, *Reasonable Faith* (Wheaton: Crossway, 2008). Each of these affirms that despite its ancient origins, the Bible remains a highly sound and authentic document.

95 The word epistemological comes from one of the Greek words for knowing. Epistemology has to do with the science and art of knowing: how we know what we know.

Word also tells us that we would only engage in such things if there were a reason to do so, and the only reason there is a reason to do so is that we live in a personal and meaningful universe created with intention and purpose by a personal and meaningful Word. Word insures that the world is worth wondering about. It enables us to see and take hold of our world with reason, thought, and rational sensibility. Word allows us to discover the essence of existence.

And, as we noted above, Word illuminates. As John writes in verses four and five (again, see the passage as it is quoted above), Word is the "light" of human beings. Word is what enlightens people, what enables them to see life clearly, what enables them to understand themselves, reality, and God. Word is the great flashlight which allows people to see life as it most and truly is. As John would have it, Word "shines" in the darkness, the darkness in which many of us live our lives, the darkness that prevents us from seeing all that life has for us, that blinds us to the larger picture of truth and meaning which is to be found in God and his profound love for us. Word opens up the fullness of reality and truth, material as well as ineffable, natural as well as supernatural. When Word speaks, Word makes clear. The speech of Word constitutes the road to comprehension and understanding. Genuine insight and lasting meaning begin with Word.

Before we go further into John's text, however, we should pause and think about a term to which we have referred often in this meditation: meaning. And when we think about what "meaning" means, we must also think about truth, for genuine meaning can only be so if it is connected to truth. Why should we believe something is meaningful if it is not really true?

Let's talk about truth first. We have already established that if Word created the world, then Word guarantees, in some way, meaning in the world. If this is so, then we must go a step further and say that Word also guarantees truth in the world. Why is this? When we look for or try to divine meaning, regardless of the occasion or circumstance, what we are really looking for is some notion of truth. We are looking for something that offers a sort of intellectual or emotional construct or point, something that, at least for the present moment, furnishes us with a working picture of or framework for how we can understand and make sense of our world. Even if it lasts for but a moment, this framework is what we consider to be our "truth," that which we believe, at least for this moment, to be a reasonably accurate encapsulation of the present significance and meaningfulness of our reality. What we find meaningful is, in some way, our "truth."

Although not all of us would say that we will one day find binding or permanent or conclusive truth, all of us would agree, I think, that what we decide is meaningful, at a given moment, is also what we believe to be most true, in a manner of speaking, in this given moment. Even if this formulation of "truth" vanishes with the next wave of insight or understanding, it is nonetheless what we believe to be "true" right now, in our immediate experience. Also, though not all of us will agree on what "truth" is or can be, we all will likely agree that whatever we may decide truth is, we will find it to be meaningful. Our notion of truth, regardless of how we define it, helps us determine what is meaningful and real to us, and what makes sense and, conversely, what does not. Although we may claim that we can experience meaning without truth, if truth did not exist, we would be hard pressed to explain what this meaning really means, and why it is meaningful. Some notion of truth, however relative or limited it may be, is essential to constructing meaning. We need a measurable and accessible starting point for evaluating our perception of reality.[96]

---

96   For a dissenting view on the possibility of truth, see the many books by Richard Rorty, including, to name just three, *Contingency, irony, and*

But what, as Pontius Pilate, the Roman procurator who sentenced Jesus to be crucified, asked shortly before he pronounced such sentence, is truth?[97]

Then, and now, this remains a very good question.

Without going into a great deal of intricate philosophical detail, let's say that truth is, generally and roughly speaking, that which corresponds to reality, that which lines up with what we believe, on our best and worst of days, is an accurate picture of our reality. If something is truth, it will agree with reality, not necessarily reality as we know, perceive, and experience it, but reality as it really is. Truth is some that faithfully represents, reflects, and explains reality as it is.[98]

Yet this invites another question: what is reality? Again, without getting lost in metaphysical muddles, let's describe reality as the total breadth of our experience. Here, however, we encounter a roadblock. Some of us will argue that reality is limited to what we can see, hear, and taste with our present senses, that whatever we learn through our senses is the sum of reality. Anything we cannot see or hear is therefore not reality.[99]

---

solidarity (New York: Cambridge University, 1969), *Objectivity, Relativism and Truth* (New York: Cambridge University, 1991), and *Philosophy and the Mirror of Nature* (Princeton, New Jersey: Princeton University, 1979) For an affirmation of the necessity of truth, see, among others, Michael P. Lynch, *True to Life: Why Truth Matters* (Cambridge, Massachusetts: MIT, 2004).

97   See John 18:35

98   For detailed expositions of this view, see Gerald Vision, *Veritas: The Correspondence Theory and Its Critics* (Cambridge, Massachusetts: MIT, 2004) as well as "The Semantic Conception of Truth" by Albert Tarski in *Truth*, edited by Simon Blackburn and Keith Simmons (Oxford: Oxford University, 1999).

99   This in turn invites another question: is reality really "real" or is it merely the product of our perceptions? Is it the "ideal" reality of Descartes or is it a reality that, as Steven Weinberg put it in a review of Hawkings's

This definition of course leaves out any notion of the metaphysical or transcendence. It omits any possibility that feelings of transcendence, those moments of unexplainable wonder and rapturous enchantment which seem to lift us beyond ourselves, have any connection to things beyond us. It would say that we experience these moments merely because we are human beings, and not because above and beyond us is a transcendent being generating them or creating the conditions that enable them to happen for us. Our physical experience is the sum of all that is existent and real.

As we have observed, however, others see reality differently. They see reality as consisting of two interconnected parts. The first part is the material world, what we see, hear, and experience with our senses. This includes physical objects as well as the way that we feel and experience them (including the feelings of temporal and transcending wonder that we discussed in relation to the first view of reality above). The second part is what we do not see, the metaphysical and ineffable: the transcendent. Reality is therefore what we see as well as what we do not (but what we nonetheless and for any number of reasons, believe exists).

If you agree with what we have concluded about the Word to this point, you are likely to agree that reality is more than what we see and hear and otherwise experience. You are likely to say that reality is multi-faceted, that it is material as well as metaphysical, transcendent, and ineffable. Indeed, you might say, as would I, that reality is a full orbed expression of a comprehensive realm of natural and, dare I add, supernatural and metaphysical experience.

Based on this view of reality, we would say that truth is

The Grand Design, "is entirely independent of us and our models"? (See "The Universes We Still Don't Know" in *The New York Review of Books*, February 10, 2011.) The larger issue is this: how much can we trust what we experience? Stay tuned.

something that effectively encompasses, explains, undergirds, and defines the material and ineffable simultaneously. Unless something explains or accounts for the presence and effects of both of these dimensions of reality, we would therefore not consider it to be truth. We would say that truth must explain and circumscribe the material as well as the immaterial in order to be effectual and, no pun intended, true.

To those who would deny this picture of truth, I will only say this: how can you know for sure? Every theory that has been advanced to define the universe has been developed within the constraints of what the universe is. None of them look at the universe from afar, but from within it. Their observation points are finite and limited. Yes, as many philosophers have demonstrated, we birth or create reality by observing it, but this does not tell us anything substantive about what we have made. We still do not know it as it is.[100]

In addition, how do we really know that there is not another, bigger reality beyond this one? Although we cannot fully prove that there may well be something outside this reality, we conversely cannot prove definitively there is not. Sure, some will say that this is an argument from silence, but so is its counterpart. It's simply replacing one argument from silence with another. It proves nothing.

On the other hand, based on our previous observations about the reasonableness and necessity of a transcendent and personal cosmological origin (including the fact of Word and all that this implies), we have every reason to conclude that reality is more likely than not to be multi-faceted and multi-dimensional. We have every reason, every logical and sensible reason to conclude that there is more to reality than, to use

---

100 In addition to Kant's observations on the impossibility of seeing "things in themselves," see John Milbank, *Theology and Social Theory* (Oxford: Blackwell, 1993), for additional thoughts on our inherent limits in grasping the essence of our reality.

an overworked phrase, meets the eye. To do otherwise is to ignore the fragility of any assertion made that suggests that the universe and all the personality in it came out of nothing. Yes, neither position is entirely provable but, clearly, only the one that holds that real reality is material *and* transcendent and metaphysical definitively explains the way the world is.[101]

And truth is that which best explains this "real" reality. To repeat, truth is a full-orbed picture of reality, one that comprises that which is visible as well as that which is invisible, one that is not so much the product of individuated perception as it is the unassailable and undeniable "givens" that are there. Truth represents and defines the real meaning of the fully coherent whole of reality, the totality of all its relevant perceptual and physical parts, a comprehensive experience of what really "is."[102]

Note, however, that even if every part of our perception agrees with each other, this does not necessarily make it true. It is only true if it accurately corresponds to reality, again, reality not as we may see it, but reality as it actually is. If we ourselves devise truth, that is, if we decide what is true, then we make truth subject to our conscious and unconscious imagination, meanderings, and whims. Truth may become what we want it to be, but not what it actually is. We have proved nothing.

Granted, these may well be the same. Indeed, if truth does

---

101 As Emily Grosholz points out in her essay "Reference and Analysis: The Representation of Time in Galileo, Newton, and Leibniz" in *The Journal of the History of Ideas, Volume 72, Number 3,* we need both concrete as well as abstract description of a given phenomenon to understand it fully. It is difficult to fully analyze reality if we are standing in it.

102 For an interesting though technical take on the idea of a "given," see Ludwig Wittgenstein's *Philosophical Investigations,* translated by G. E. M. Anscombe (Oxford: Blackwell, 1953, 2001).

indeed fully represent our reality, and if we experience that reality, then truth will very likely be something that, in some mysterious way, becomes what we believe or instinctively feel most fully corresponds to our ideas of what is reasonable and accurate about our experience. On the other hand, if we make truth *only* what we perceive it to be, we run the risk of making it something that it is not. We will only be affirming what we have already decided must be right, without any recourse to independent examination or study. We do not bother with a hypothesis, but go directly to theory.

Truth must be something that transcends all our individual definitions without denying that we have come to them. It must be something that is always real and certain, regardless of what we think. It must encompass, comprise, define, and explain reality apart from whatever else we may conclude about it. It must offer a permanent and final definition of what is meaningful and real. Truth must be a universal which is a universal regardless of whatever else we may determine to be sensible or real.

Hence, truth is more likely something that we discover or discern, not something that we create. For instance, did Isaac Newton decide that gravity existed, or did he discover that it existed? Yes, Newton may have determined that something like gravity was necessary to ensuring the integrity of the world as people perceived and experienced it, but he did not "make" gravity out of the blue. It was there all along. Newton "discovered" gravity after studying the evidence that gravity had, through the workings of Newton's reality, presented to him of its existence.

In addition, truth must be unique. If there is more than one truth, nothing is truth, for the truth must necessarily be the *only* conclusion that we can draw about the nature of reality (if we all developed our own notions of truth, how would we know which one is most "true"?). Truth cannot be divided or subsumed into something else. Truth must always be what it is—and only what it is.

Let us then establish that truth must be something, be it a proposition, judgment, or agreement that is consistent with one, the given, verifiable, and accurately established facts of reality; and two, the human perception of those facts of reality. For this reason, although apart from the exercise of religious faith, we may find proving what is absolutely "true" truth to be extremely difficult (for even faith, if it is to be rational and reasonable, requires a foundation to be materially valid, a point to which we will return eventually), we can nonetheless conclude that one, truth, in as absolute a sense as finitude allows, exists; two, we humans can know it; and three, to repeat an earlier point, it must agree with what is perceptible and real. It must be consistent with what is definitively "there".[103]

Truth will therefore be as fullest a picture of reality as we can discern.[104]

---

103 Before we proceed further, we should note that unless reality is something that we experience, it is not a reality in which we participate. Although there could be other realities, those need not concern us, for we are not a part of them, at least not consciously. And it is our conscious experience on which we are focusing, and it is our conscious experience that we are trying to define and for which we are endeavoring to present an idea of truth.

104 Of course it goes without saying that whichever definition of reality we choose, we make truth frightfully dependent on our perception, and our perception may not always, at a given moment, accurately assess the state of the world around us. Yet we must trust our perception. What else do we have to determine the shape of what we experience? Yes, some of us will perceive a multi-layered reality, and some of us will not. Does this mean that one of our perceptual mechanisms is faulty? Of course not: it merely means that some of us have chosen to conclude and believe that, on the basis of the evidence available to all of us, we perceive things that others do not. Yet our perception does not create reality; reality would exist regardless of whether and how we perceive it. Our perception simply

Before thinking about meaning, let's try to connect these thoughts to Word. Recall first that we observed that, on the basis of the initial verses of John's gospel, Word exists, completely, totally, and absolutely as an eternal presence amidst and beyond the cosmos. It is not dependent upon our belief or disbelief in it to be the eternal presence that it is. Word will be Word whether or not we ever acknowledge that it is there. Also, we noted that Word, and nothing else, created the universe. Everything that is owes its existence to Word.

In addition, we noted that, as its creator, Word defines and orders reality, and gives it meaning, value, and purpose. Word encompasses the entirety of reality, its natural as well as its supernatural dimensions. Word also explains the entirety of reality, explains why reality is the way it is, why we are the way we are, why the world is a personal place inhabited by personal beings. Word is the fullest definition and definer of what is.

What can we conclude from this? Simply, Word is truth. Word is the fullest explanation for and most complete foundation of reality and how we perceive it. It is the starting point for explicating what is most real. Whether we develop our own notions of truth doesn't matter. Word remains the seminal and unique truth, the truth from which all of our other truths, regardless of how we come to or define them, come. It is all the truth that can possibly be truth.

Now let's address the notion of meaning. Where would we be without meaning?

We would be nowhere. We cannot live without meaning. Consider an experiment done with a group of college students

---

determines how we view and experience reality. Hence, some people will believe in the transcendent because they believe they have experienced it, whereas others will reject such belief because they do not believe they can or will experience it.

recently. Researchers gave these students two choices. Would they like to live in a perfectly tuned environment, an environment absent of all problems and heartaches, but an environment in which they had no opportunity to discover anything about it? Or would they prefer to live in an environment with headaches, problems, and challenges, yet an environment which they could manipulate, explore, and touch every moment they were in it?

Most of the students opted for the second choice. Why? They would rather live in a world in which they could find and discover things, rather than a world, although it is devoid of problems, offers no hope for finding a meaningful way to live in it. They wanted to feel and know meaning, any kind of meaning; they wanted to know that they were more than well manicured robots in a sterile and seemingly safe environment. Regardless of the challenges that attended living in an openended way, they wanted to know that, if they wished to do so, they could live in a manner that allowed them to find out why they were alive and here in the world. They wanted to know that they could find meaning.[105]

As do we. We all live for meaning.

Think about as well the work of Victor Frankel, a German psychologist who studied the experiences of survivors of the twentieth century Nazi concentration camps. Frankel consistently observed that despite the panoply of horrors and hardship in the camps, the inmates nonetheless sought to rise above their situation and to, in every circumstance, seek—and find—meaning in it. They strove to feel as if life

---

105 Consider also a recent study on college students and spirituality done by the High Education Research Institute at the Graduate School of Education and Information Studies at the University of California at Los Angeles. Like the rest of us, college students, this study concluded, long for spiritual, however they define it, meaning. They want to know they can invest and fill their lives with a deeper, transcendent purpose.

was worth it. Despite the pain of their existence, they wanted it to be meaningful, wanted it to be an experience in which they could find purpose, value, and hope.

So do we. Despite any problems we may encounter in the course of our lives, we want our lives to be purposeful, to have a point. We want our lives to have meaning. To seek meaning is the basic bent of humanity, the common drive compelling every human being to live each day. We all desire it. We all desire a sense of satisfaction and wholeness in our lives, something that makes life worth living. We all want to feel as though our lives have a reason, to feel as if what we do, think, or experience is satisfying and valuable, even in a very small way. Even if we all are, as Sartre put it, "useless passions," we nonetheless all wish to find contentment and purpose in our lives. We all want meaning.[106]

Moreover, though we may claim, as do Sartre and the existentialists, that life has no meaning, we end up contradicting ourselves, every moment of every day. We will still live as though we appreciate meaning, as though we want our existence to be satisfying and fulfilling. We will still seek to make our time on this planet valuable and worthwhile, even if it is only for ourselves and no one else. We will still strive to find hope. Otherwise, if we are to be absolutely consistent with ourselves, we would end our lives tonight. What would be the point of us being here?

Indeed, though Paolo, the protagonist of Thomas Mann's novella *The Will for Happiness,* died once his "will for happiness" had been satisfied, the reason he did so was because he "no longer had a pretext for living." Oddly, for him, the time at which he found meaning became the time

---

106 See Victor E. Frankel, *Man's Search for Meaning* (New York: Pocket Books, 1984).

for him to lose it. To find meaning was to actually not find it at all. And so his life ended that very day.[107]

But Paolo still needed and wanted meaning.

Also, to say that there is no meaning is to say that, ironically, there *is* meaning. Our denial of meaning becomes our meaning. The rejection of meaning becomes the acceptance of it. Those who most vehemently deny life has no meaning therefore turn out to be the ones who need it most. All else aside, they still need to believe that they are important and significant, still need to believe that they have value. What else would they do?

We cannot have it both ways. Either the universe has meaning and we who live in it have meaning, too, or the universe has no meaning and we who live in it do not have meaning, either. But wait: if the universe has no meaning, if it has no reason to be here, then why would it contain beings who have and desire meaning? Unless the universe is meaningful, there is no reason for us to exist and look for meaning in it, anyway. Indeed, there is no reason for *anything*.

Yes, we can think about chaos theory or the various multiverse theories of origins, which hold that the way the world is, given all possibilities and inevitabilities, the only way that it could be. Regardless of how neat and clever these pictures may be, however, they still fail to answer the question of *why* all this mass of potential universe was around to begin with. Where is the meaning?[108]

Hence, unless we wish to lapse into a morass of dead ends from which we cannot escape, we must consider ourselves as creatures who are living in a universe with meaning,

107 Thomas Mann, *The Will for Happiness* in *Death in Venice and Other Tales,* translated by Joachim Neugroschel (New York: Viking, 1998).

108 On chaos theory, see, among others, Graham Masterton, *Chaos Theory* (New York: Severn House, 2007).

regardless of where and how we might find it. Absent this, existentialism's thesis of the authenticating act that finds meaning is patently absurd. It simply can't happen. In a meaningless universe, what is the point?

Again: it is impossible to live without meaning.[109]

But now we ask the question once more. What is meaning? This is a difficult question, for all of us have different notions of what is meaningful or what it feels to experience meaning. Depending on our background, upbringing, geographic location, cultural loci, or genetics, we find meaning in many, many different ways. We are unique persons with unique personalities, interests, and desires.

Nonetheless, let us affirm at the outset that in addition to being a compendium of all possibilities for human flourishing, meaning is a sense of satisfaction or fulfillment, something that in some way, shape, or form, meets, at a given moment, our essential or desired human need for value or worth. Meaning is what gives our lives value, meaning is what makes our lives purposeful and worth living. We live for meaning, we live with meaning, we live *by* meaning. Indeed, we would hope that we die with meaning, too.[110]

---

109 Recall our earlier comments about Albert Camus's observation that because people do not wish to come to grips with life's inherent senselessness, they go on living as if it makes sense, anyway, as if, despite its absurdity, it has meaning. They really have no choice. The alternative is death and the end of everything they know.

110 This of course raises a problem. Who or what determines what it means to flourish? Moreover, how does morality relate to flourishing? Do we need to define the essence of flourishing with religion or, alternatively, with neurons? For more on this, see Sam Harris, *The Moral Landscape* (New York: Free Press, 2010), which argues that meaning and morality are specifically neuronal and that religion or any level of transcendent spirituality is not necessary to make this determination. Harris contends that a value is a fact, and that we can therefore construct our moral system solely on the basis of empirical experience. In contrast, see the recently

But what is the satisfaction of meaning? Again, though it varies from person to person, the satisfaction of meaning is ultimately what a person finds most true and real for herself, what a person decides most decisively gives her a reasonable and sensible way to find pleasure and purpose in existence. It is what makes a person's life full, complete, and worth living. Meaning's satisfaction, whether it be reasonable, perverted, or something else altogether, keeps people going each day. It is the goal of their existence.[111]

(It of course goes without saying that part of meaning is to believe that we can find meaning. Somehow and some way, we believe that we can find meaning, believe that we can find

---

established "God and Human Flourishing" project in the Yale Center for Faith and Culture at Yale University and its efforts to understand the integral link between faith and human flourishing. Although its initial conclusions are tentative, they nonetheless seem to indicate that faith plays an essential role in a person's perception of her experience of flourishing. In addition, as David Eagleman notes in his *Incognito,* neuroimaging may not always yield fail safe determinations of the basis of behavior (*Incognito: The Secret Lives of the Brain* (New York: Pantheon, 2011)). Hence, we might observe that there yet remains a mystery in ascertaining precisely how we come into and experience morality. Indeed, why are we moral?

111 Although in using the term "perverted" we run into accusations of moral exclusivity, it is clear that most of us agree on some standards for such things. For instance, most people would consider the actions of the late serial murderer Ted Bundy, a man who confessed to killing thirty women before his execution in 1989, or the equally sordid activities of the late Aileen Wuornos, executed in 2002 for killing seven men she met in the course of her travels in the state of Florida, fall into the category of a satisfaction which most of us would consider illegitimate. Meaning may well be in the "eye of the beholder," but as we shall see, such a definition of meaning creates a meaning that ultimately means nothing at all. The writings of Marquis de Sade illustrate this point amply. As he wrote in *Justine,* "What will become … of morality" when life is reduced to a "current of fluid?" See Marquis de Sade, *Justine* (Chicago: Wilder Press, 2009).

in this life a measure of personal satisfaction. We believe in positive outcomes. Otherwise, why would we bother?)

Yet if meaning varies from person to person, and if meaning is found in countless and diverse ways, some of which most of us, as we observed in the footnote above, would consider highly perverse, can we really decide on one ultimate meaning? Is there one meaning that somehow exceeds or supersedes or embodies all the others, some meaning that enables us to make sense of what true meaning *really* is?

Let us first note that true meaning must arise from accurate and truthful perceptions of reality. Apart from an accurate correspondence to what is real, meaning means nothing. Illusion may be comforting, but it will ultimately disappoint. It's not realistic, and it is certainly not real. At its best, meaning must rise out of all real and verifiable possibilities at hand. And recognizing all the possibilities at hand means that we must accept that, as we did when we discussed the nature of truth, the scope of possibilities for meaning encompasses not only our material experience, but our immaterial experiences as well. To properly delineate meaning we must therefore analyze both. We must agree that true meaning is to be found by examining what is physically present as well as what is not, that we must consider physical *and* metaphysical experience as we look to understand what meaning most is.

We all know, however, that any one of us can find meaning in this world and this world alone. We all know that we do not need to believe in transcendence to find satisfaction and happiness in this existence. Right here, right now, we all can find meaning. Right here, right now, we all can find something that we will find to be joyous and satisfying. This world contains a nearly inexhaustible fount of options for meaning; it is a cornucopia of value and purpose for every human sensibility. Very few people ever feel left out. Indeed, we can spend our entire lives enjoying this planet's various moments without ever believing that we need anything more for meaning than what is before us, without us ever requiring transcendence or an ultimate vision to pull our lives together. Indeed, even if we find them to be disjointed, disconnected, or not always apparent, we can nonetheless believe that the meanings and satisfactions of this world are sufficient for us. We can live and die solely with and in the meaning of this world. As David Peterson puts it, "this world is all we need."[112]

Yet if we are to be honest about our assessment of the world, we must admit that although we can find joy and value and meaning in the things of this world, we cannot unequivocally say that these things in themselves constitute all the meaning that we can define, experience, or find. How can we? As we concluded that, in regard to truth, we need a larger framework of possibility to fully grasp truth in our temporal experience, so we must acknowledge that we need a bigger picture of meaning to give genuine substance to the meaning that we experience in the here and now. We need an objective way to evaluate what we find. To this end, we must admit that meaning only has real value if the world itself has meaning. And the only way that a nameless and faceless world has meaning is if something bigger than it ensures that it does. A random world cannot, in itself, give itself meaning. In a universe of capricious and indefinable origins, there is none to be had.

To wit, as we have already concluded earlier in this meditation, we therefore look to transcendence and the metaphysical, however we define them, to ensure, articulate, and affirm genuine and full meaning in our lives. We do so

---

112 See David Peterson, *On the Wild Edge: In Search of a Natural Life* (New York: H. Holt, 2005).

because we believe that the meanings of this world are only meaningful if above and beyond this world is a transcendence that is in some way undergirding, integrating, and pulling together our various and assorted experiences of joy and meaning into a larger picture of meaning, a picture of permanent and lasting meaning. We believe that meaning is not meaning without transcendence (and, for many of us, a personal transcendence at that), and that we need such transcendence to make sense of things as we see them in the here and now. To suppose that, as finite beings we can see beyond our momentary flashes of insight and engagement to understand what they really are, is to stir up and serve a stew of our own deliberations without having a credible recipe to do so.

Yes, we affirm that we must construct meaning based on present experience, and yes, we acknowledge that meaning must arise out of our common exchange with the phenomena of the world. Yet we also insist that if this is the *only* way that we construct meaning, we bump into the dilemma we posed earlier: how do we know it?

More importantly, how can we prove it?

Again, although concluding that finitude is the sole beginning, end, and repository of meaning recognizes the fact of human mortality, it overlooks that the finite mind born into that mortality cannot conceive of all possibilities available to it precisely because it cannot know whether it has actually experienced all of them. As any skeptic (and non-skeptic as well) will readily agree (or at least *ought* to agree!), finitude simply cannot know all things.

The bottom line is therefore this: a random and finite world will never have real meaning.

What can we do? We must ground real meaning in real truth, the real truth about the way the world and reality are. And the real truth about the way the world and reality are, is, as we have observed, grounded in the fact and presence of Word. Word is the ultimate truth of reality.

And Word is therefore the ultimate ground of meaning. As the world's creator, Word is the foundation upon which and the framework within which meaning is discovered, surmised, and constructed within it. While we can claim that meaning, as well as truth, will vary from creature to creature depending on how it interprets its experience in the world and the many structures and patterns that comprise it, we cannot claim that meaning is ever independent of these structures. As the creator, Word has constructed these conditions and structures. It is Word's creative work that enables meaning to be and to be found. Word ensures that we can find meaning, and Word ensures that we can even think about meaning. It also ensures that we will wonder *why* and, in particular, ensures that we will wonder why we are even here to be meaningful. Meaning begins and ends with the eternal creator Word. Word is meaning.[113]

And Word is a meaning that does not vary from person to person. It will always be meaningful to everyone in the same way. Word's meaning is not based on relative standards, standards that shift from culture to culture and place to place, but on an enduring and permanent point: the fact of Word as creator of the world. Hence, although we all have different experiences and satisfactions which we consider meaningful

---

113 We should also note that, and we will enlarge on this later, unless meaning and truth reveal themselves in such a way that no one would mistake them for anything other than *the* meaning and *the* truth, they would still be elusive. We may pinpoint their relevance for our lives; we may ascertain their specificity in various situations; and we may decide what might constitute them; but we could not really know them as they are. Validating our knowing and therefore our truth and meaning depends on our perceiving and experiencing truth and meaning as they really are (and to know that they are as such).

(as we should; life would be rather boring if we all enjoyed exactly the same things for exactly the same reasons), we must understand that ultimately we do so because of Word's existence and presence in the world. Everything we know as meaningful is meaningful because of the fact of Word.

To repeat, without Word, there is no meaning, and without Word, our diverse and sundry satisfactions would have no point. Life would be hopeless, an achingly and thoroughly—in the broadest possible sense—unexplainable beingness without rational start, reason, or end.

Existential fulfillment and satisfaction begin with Word.

Let's summarize where we have been so far. As we thought about how Word creates, informs, and illuminates humankind, we turned to consider the essence of meaning and truth. We subsequently established that truth must accurately reflect all parts and facets of reality. We also decided that if we are to be realistic about reality, we will acknowledge that reality must include all possible parameters of experience, including the metaphysical and supernatural. As to meaning, we concluded that meaning must also reflect all possible parameters of experience, material as well as immaterial. Furthermore, we decided that if we are to experience meaning in a meaningful way, we must connect it to truth. Without truth, meaning has no basis. Finally, we observed that although we can determine how to define truth or what might comprise truth, the "truest" truth is something that is true whether we believe it to be so or not. It is also true regardless of whether we are aware of it being so. Truth is something that is always there, even if we are not.

Most importantly, we established that, on the basis of its position as the uncaused personal and eternal creator of all things, Word is truth, the beginning of all real form and possibility in the universe, the truth that is always true regardless of what anyone imagines or thinks. Moreover, if Word is the starting point of truth, then it is also the starting point of meaning, the meaning that, although we experience it in this world, finds its ultimate roots in what is beyond this world, the personal metaphysical presence (Word) from which it has come. In Word we see the definition and beginning of truth and meaning in our experience, the foundation of all purpose and enjoyment in existence. Word is the essential ground of what truth is and what it means, the ultimate illumination and enlightenment, the final satisfaction of existence. As the eternal αρχη, Word is the infinite source of all that is meaningful and true, the sustaining uncaused cause and progenitor and circumscriber of truth and meaning in the cosmos. In Word we see the beginning of everything of substance and value in the universe.

Again: insight, truth, wisdom, and meaning begin in Word.

As we noted in a recent footnote, however, we still face a considerable challenge. If Word is truth and meaning, how can we know this truth and meaning? How can we encounter them in our experience? We believe that as the eternal and uncaused beginning, Word created us, that as the source of life and existence Word endowed the universe with meaning and purpose, and that as the ultimate point of illumination Word is the source of all that is valuable and true. But we do not yet know how we can *experience* Word, how we can directly experience Word as these things. We do not yet know how we can experience Word as the personal illumination and decisive truth and meaning that undergird, define, and pervade the universe and our experience as personal beings in it. How do we get to know the speech that birthed the universe?

Right away, however, we see a problem. If we believe that Word is ultimate meaning and truth as well as that which is eternal and beyond our immediate comprehension, we have no good way to get to know Word, this ineffable and eternal speech of meaning and truth. We have no way to really taste it and what it can be for us. How do we get to know the truth, the truth expressed in the speech that created the cosmos, if it is centered in a realm beyond our ken?

In short, how can an independent and self-aware creator move into and speak to its creation in a way that the creation understands it while it—the creator—remains an eternal and self-existent creator Word? How can truth remain truth while becoming part of what it gives truth to? If truth lives in what it makes true, how can it really give truth to it? How can the creator remain its eternal self while being organically involved in the creation?

On the one hand, this seems an impossible task. How can the infinite and eternal become limited and bound by time, part of our finite and temporal experience? How can the creator become part of its creation? Also, even if it could, how could it do so without disrupting the entire created order? How can we see the infinite and eternal in our earthly experience without destroying that experience altogether?[114] It's like trying to fit a powerful northeaster wind, the type that moved the hurricanes portrayed so powerfully in Sebastian Junger's *The Perfect Storm,* into a box. How does one go about doing such a thing? Boundaries are meant for things that can be bound. As any aficionado of monster movies knows, humans have much difficulty taming or mastering creatures that originate from beyond the earthly realm.[115]

---

114 Note that there is a difference between being infinite and being infinity, and a difference between being eternal and eternity. God is eternal, but God is not eternity, and God is infinite, but he is not infinity. He creates and sustains them, but them he *is* not.

115 See Junger's *Perfect Storm: A True Story of Men Against the Sea* (New York: Norton, 1997) as well as the movie of the same name, released in 2000 by Warner Bros. Pictures.

On the other hand, Word is personal. As a personal being, would it not therefore wish to communicate with the creation, the personal creation it made? Do not we who are parents seek to communicate with our children, those whom we brought into the world? Of course: personal beings are made and inclined to interact and communicate with each other. Yet Word has a big problem. It is a personal being who wishes to interact with the personal beings in the personal creation it made, yet it realizes it cannot readily do so without dismantling the very creation that these personal beings enjoy.

How is Word to proceed? We can think of some possibilities almost immediately. Maybe we can picture Word as akin to the Hindu Brahman, the vast and unconditioned presence that contains, births, and enables all things to be while remaining all things in itself. Or perhaps we can envision Word as Paul Tillich's "ground of being," an amorphous beingness from which everything has come and which continues to uphold all things while not necessarily being apart from them. Or maybe we can posit Word as the god of a Christian theological trend called process theology, a god that moves and changes with its creation. Perhaps we can see Word as a deistic god, a god that creates, then walks away from what it had made. Or maybe we can represent Word as the creator of the ancient Gnostics, a creator whose creation is simply an extension, however, distant and convoluted, of itself.[116]

None of these answers, however, are satisfactory. Clearly, a creator that is not separate from its creation cannot in truth be an uncaused beginning of all things, for it cannot create

---

116 See Tillich's *Systematic Theology, Volume One* (Chicago: University of Chicago, 1951), and John B. Cobb, Jr. and David Ray Griffin, *Process Theology* (Philadelphia: Westminster, 1976).

without being a part of what it makes. It requires the creation to be what it is in itself. This creator will not adequately explain how the beginning "began." The only creator that can be an uncaused beginning of its creation is a creator that has always been separate and apart from its creation. Although this creator may or may not participate in its creation, if it is to be the genuine origin of this creation it must certainly, at the beginning, be apart from it. It cannot be what it creates. To be a genuinely distinctive and omnipotent creator, Word must therefore be separate and distinctive, in essence, from its creation.[117]

Yet the point remains: Word is personal. So what do we do?

Bottom line, what we are asking is this. How can a cause, an uncaused personal cause at that, become a temporary and limited ("caused") effect? If Word is ultimate cause, it cannot be effect. Although it can effect, that is, although it can "cause" effects, it itself cannot be an effect, for it cannot be "caused." If Word were to become cause *and* effect, then Word would not only "cause" effects but also become the effects that it causes.

Yet this is the natural rhythm of the universe. Every effect has a cause and, unless the universe suddenly stops functioning, every effect becomes a new cause. In the big picture, all causes become effects, and all effects become causes.[118]

---

117 We are assuming here a universe which God (Word) and creation occupy jointly, although God (Word) is not an organic (material) part of it).

118 We might also think about the idea, drawn from the work of the philosopher G. W. F. Hegel and given different form by Johann Gottlieb Fichte, of characterizing history as a process of a thesis that interacts with a antithesis, out of which comes a synthesis, which in turns becomes a new thesis to a new antithesis and so to a new synthesis, and so on. All

Consider, for instance, a rain cloud. When a rain cloud has accumulated sufficient moisture, it drops it to the earth as rain or some other form of precipitation (snow, hail, etc.). Once the cloud releases its moisture, it dissipates. Its days as a cause are over. When the cloud's moisture (its effect) hits the earth, however, it eventually, perhaps over a very long period of time, finds its way back to the sky to form part of a new rain cloud. The effect thus becomes a cause. As the first law of thermodynamics states, the total amount of matter and energy in the universe is constant. Every cause can thus potentially become an effect, and every effect can potentially become a cause.[119]

Let us note, however, that without cause, we have no possibility; but without effects, we have no actuality. If the personal Word as uncaused cause therefore became an effect, though we would have its actuality, we would no longer have its presence as possibility, at least not in an infinite sense. We would lose our infinite and uncaused beginning. Yet if this personal Word wishes to communicate itself most clearly with the personal beings it made, it needs to become the effect that they are, an organic part of what it had made. Word as infinite possibility would need to become finite actuality while continuing to be infinite possibility.

How can this be? How can something that has always existed become something that exists, something that is born, lives, and dies? How can something that exists beyond all agency of cause and effect become subject to it, tossed to and

---

present things become part of future things. (Hegel used the terminology of Abstract, Negative, Concrete.)

119 As the character John Ames puts it in the novel *Gilead,* "I read somewhere that a thing that does not exist in relation to anything else cannot itself be said to exist." See Marilynne Robinson, *Gilead* (London: Virago Press, 2005). Everything is interconnected, everything is interrelated, and everything flows out of the other.

fro by it as it travels through the various warps, twists, and turns of the universe even while it is sustaining this universe? Word is not a rain cloud, an actuality becoming a possibility over and over again. It is infinite, the uncaused cause. And how can an uncaused cause be subject to causation? How can that which has not been caused *be* caused?

There is another problem, one to which we alluded earlier. If Word as uncaused cause occupies space or physicality of any kind, which we assume that, in some way, it must, then if it stops being an eternal and infinite uncaused cause to become an effect, what happens to the space and timelessness it once occupied and sustained? Do they shrink? Do they disappear? Does something else keep space and time going? Furthermore, given that Word as uncaused cause is responsible, in some way, for how its creation functions, what happens to the creation when its creator becomes part of it? Does its creator still watch over it? Does its creator still superintend it? Does its creator still work in it?

Put another way, what will happen to the creation when, as George Berkeley speculated, no one is thinking about or perceiving it? Can it still exist?[120]

In addition, even if we assume that the creation could continue on its own and that the infinite could be bound in the finite, we must still ask what this would look like. How would a material and finite infinite (the ultimate paradox, it seems) appear to be? How would we perceive it in our reality? How would we experience it?

Clearly, if Word is to become an effect, and if the universe is to retain its integrity, Word must remain the uncaused cause. The λογος must remain the αρχη. Yet if we are to experience Word as it is, Word must be a finite and personal effect, a *bio* (a

---

120 See George Berkeley, *The Principles of Human Knowledge*, edited by G. J. Warnock (London: Collins, 1962).

life), a visible and subjective point in temporal reality. Unless Word presents itself in this way, we are forced to admit that we are living in a universe brought to life, a personal and rich and dynamic life, by an uncaused cause that we will never really know, and that we are aware of an ultimate truth and meaning but equally aware that we will never know them in full. The truth and meaning of all being will forever elude us, forever existing apart from definitive mortal perception.

Yes, we can decide that this uncaused cause is there, that it indeed established the world and brought it to life, that it conveys all substantial and adequate meaning for our lives. We can even attempt to communicate with it, try to formulate a way to bring it into our experience. And maybe we will. But we will never know for certain that we are really doing so. Though we may believe that we are reaching out to something, may believe that we are making a connection, we will never know for sure. All that we will have will be our dreams and hopes about it, our imaginings about our decidedly unproven experience of the metaphysical and divine. It would be like worshipping a wooden idol. We will never definitively know whether we are experiencing and communicating with what we believe to be the genesis of all life and being.[121]

But maybe we don't need to know such things. Maybe we do not need to know what is beyond us. Maybe we should simply live our lives on the basis of what we think we know and be content with it. Maybe, as did the Greeks, we should just assume, as without any evidence, that this uncaused cause is out there, up there, a lifeless but epistemologically necessary center of meaning, and live out our lives as we see

---

121 For some insightful thoughts on the inutility of worshipping idols, see the story of Elijah and the prophets of Baal on Mt. Carmel (1 Kings 18) as well as the prophet Isaiah's ruminations on idols in the forty-fourth chapter of his lengthy prophetic vision.

fit. Or maybe we should forget that such a thing might even exist. Absent any firm physical evidence for it, why not?[122]

On the other hand, if we know, on the basis of good evidence, that somewhere there exists a personal being, a thinking and feeling personal being who as uncaused cause spawned and endowed this cosmos with life, order, personality, and meaning, a being to whom we therefore owe our very purpose, wouldn't we, if we could, want to know it personally? Wouldn't we want to know it in our experience, to understand it more fully and intimately? Would we not want to know the truth and meaning that undergird and explain our lives, the ultimate purpose that this uncaused cause presents and contains? I think we'd be less than human if we did not. As I said at the outset of this book, everyone has and retains a sense of wonder, a longing for more, a compulsion to know beyond the present moment, to understand whatever she does not presently grasp in her life. And as we have noted time and time again, everyone looks for truth and meaning, of some kind, in their lives. *Everyone*. We all want to know the meaning of the speech of the universe, the answer to the riddle of why we are here, the key to understanding our meaning, value, and purpose. Although we may pursue this quest in a variety of ways, we cannot avoid pursuing it altogether. We cannot avoid investigating the content and value of our physical and, for most of us, metaphysical boundaries.

If we can accept (as we should) that this is who we are, then we can perhaps also accept that, all things considered, we will wish to know, on a personal level, this personal and infinite uncaused cause in our lives. We will wish to know the starting point of reality.

---

122 As we have observed, the Greeks believed that, even if they could not physically prove it, the λογος was necessary to proper knowledge— proper epistemological understanding—of reality.

Yet herein lies the mystery, the mystery that has perplexed countless generations of human beings: how can we know what we by nature cannot (and logically should not) know? How can the personal infinite become something that we who are personal, yet finite, may understand?

Again: how can what is infinite and personal become finite and personal?

Ironically, though we may want to know the infinite, we may not accept that the only way we can know it is to embrace what seems to be a logical impossibility for it to become. Therefore, either we suspend our life long understanding of the nature of the infinite or we decide that we will from this point believe something about it which we never thought we could or should. We decide to believe something about the infinite without fully knowing how or why we can do so.

Why should we do this? We do it because we realize that ultimately, as we noted in talking about Ecclesiastes 3:11, we live our lives in a mystery, a mystery whose solutions lie in realms and thoughts far beyond our own. Oddly (and paradoxically) enogh, we must accept things that we do not readily understand if we are to begin to understand things as they are.[123]

The issue then becomes one of faith. How much do we want to believe without seeing? How much do we want to believe without having consistent confirmation and proof of it? How much do we want to believe without ever knowing it with physical certainty?

On the one hand, this is the nature of faith. If we knew everything, we wouldn't need faith. Faith is what enables us to embrace and trust what we cannot prove but which

---

123 We are reminded here of Augustine's famous observation that, "I believe in order to understand," as well as that of Anselm (archbishop of Canterbury in the eleventh century) that, "he who has not experienced will not understand."

we nonetheless believe, on the basis of solid and testable evidence, objective as well as subjective, to be true. It is the boundary between what we can see and what we cannot, the dividing line that spans what seems evident but what we cannot empirically prove.

Faith in the inevitability of unseen truth is very similar to the way that we believe that two plus two equals four. Can we prove that two plus two equals four? Not really; it is a fundamental assumption that we make about the nature of numbers. Or what about the assertion that a right triangle always contains one angle that is ninety degrees? Can we prove this? Again, not really; we simply understand that this is the nature of a right triangle.[124]

On the other hand, there is faith, and there is faith. Faith in faith for faith's sake means nothing. We are crazy to believe something simply to believe it. Reasonable faith, the faith that we as finite people ought to explore, invoke, and pursue, however, is faith that has a firm and verifiable basis, faith that has sound evidence and ground, faith that, because of what it has faith in, is, to use the philosopher Alvin Plantinga's words, "properly basic" to the way we see the world. It is faith with a meaningful foundation, point of entry, and established veracity.[125]

If we can therefore find solid evidence that Word did indeed become an effect, if we can find unmistakable evidence that the personal and infinite Word did indeed insert itself into our finite reality, then we would have a credible reason for believing that it did so. We would not believe simply

---

124 If this seems difficult to accept, consider that no less a mind than Bertrand Russell also had similar misgivings. Why, he asked, must we accept these axioms without proof? See his memoir, *The Autobiography of Bertrand Russell* (Boston: Little & Brown, 1967).

125 See Plantinga's *Warranted Christian Belief* (New York: Oxford, 2000).

because we want to or because it seems the easiest thing to do, but because after reviewing all the evidence, we believe that, if we are to decipher the full meaning of our lives, it is the most reasonable and rational thing to do.

We think here, once more, of paradox. To be known, the infinite must become finite; yet if it becomes finite it ceases to be infinite. How do we proceed?

Once again, however, John seems to have anticipated our trajectory and the problems it raises. As we shall see, he will now, steadily and bit by bit unfold Word to us even more, slowly dismantling Word's distance and transcendence, carefully dissembling Word's ethereality and mystery to the point where we, mere mortals, will see Word as it is, will see it as fully as it can possibly be in our material experience. In time, John will enable us to see, to physically see the essence of the divine, the essential character of the speech that birthed the cosmos and everything in it, the truth and meaning of all reality

In so doing, John will present the decisive point of his argument, the point which will enable us to finally answer the question: how do we see Word? How do we see our creator? How do we grasp the meaning of the universe? How do we see and engage the ultimate truth of the cosmos?

It all comes down to verse 14. In John 14, we see the linchpin of John's argument. Before we discuss it, let's put it, as well as some of the verses that immediately follow it, on the page:

> "And the Word became flesh, and dwelt among us, full of grace and truth. And we saw his glory, glory as of the only begotten of the Father, full of grace and truth. John testified about Him and cried out, saying, 'This was He of whom I said, 'He who comes

after me has a higher rank than I, for He existed before me. For of his fullness we have received, and grace upon grace. For the Law was given through Moses; grace and truth came to be in Jesus Christ. No one has seen God at any time; the only begotten God who is in the bosom of the Father, he has explained him." (John 1:14-18).

As John states, "Word became flesh." Word, that is, God, the creator of the universe and all that is within it, Word, the beginning and framer of truth and meaning, *became* flesh, became existentially viable, a flesh and blood person—like any other human being—in the material reality that it created, a singular and unmistakable point in what it had made. Word took on earthly form and substance and adopted the earth bound mantle of the space and time that it had made. Word lived in the reality that it birthed. Its eternal presence became concretely perceptible and spatial and temporal in the world. What had been a transcendent mystery now became an immanent fullness, a material something that it had not been before, yet a material something like any other material something. The metaphysical became physical, the supernatural the natural. Time and eternity came together.

In short, the text is saying, God became a human being. God became a person like you and me—one of us—a personal being exactly like the personal beings in the personal universe he made.[126] The infinite Word became a finite human being, the uncaused cause now a caused effect. The eternal became temporal, the beginning of all things an end in what it created.

---

126 Consider as well the song by Joan Osborne of the same name, written by Rick Bazilian and featured on Ms. Osborne's album *Relish,* released in 1995 on Blue Gorilla and Mercury records.

Journey and destiny came together, that which gives life now inextricably linked to death, infinite and finite coalescing in profound (and clearly inscrutable) exchange. What seemed to be impossible not only became possible, but found actuality in living and breathing form. The speech that birthed the universe was before us. Communication had come full circle.[127]

More profound words have never been written: God became a human being, a specific and singular human being, enshrined, as Milton puts it in *Paradise Regained*, "in fleshly tabernacle and human form."[128]

And this being had a name. This name was, John goes on to say, Jesus (see verse 29). In Jesus, Word became flesh, rests the ultimate meeting of human and divine, the final and crowing nexus of cause and effect. In Jesus, truth and meaning became visibly and palpably present in the human experience.[129]

Put another way, in Jesus, God, the almighty and unlimited creator, became as mortal and frail as you and me, as subject to physical disability and limitation as anyone else, as much a potential victim of death as anyone who has ever lived. Yet he fully remained the living and eternal God, continually expressing God's presence and personal goodness in the creation while constantly affirming who God really is. In Jesus, God became part of our world. The eternal bedrock

---

127 In addition, although God had once been outside of time, unilaterally ushering the world into existence, now he began to *experience* it.

128 John Milton, *Paradise Regained* (New York: W. W. Norton, 1975).

129 The name Greek name Jesus is based on the Hebrew word *yesua,* which means "savior." As the gospel writers saw and presented him, Jesus was the savior of the world, the one whom God sent to bring life and meaning (or put another way, salvation, a word which means in turn "rescue," a rescue, in this case, from sin, a point to which we will return) to humanity.

of the universe entered into the temporality of its physical structures and constitution. The eternal speech became that which was temporally spoken: foundational meaning became a brick in that which it grants meaning, speaking and affirming what it had already spoken into existence. In Jesus, whom Martin Luther poetically called the "mirror of God," we see God as he is, see him as fully as we possibly can in our immediate physical and material experience. In short, simply and directly, Jesus is God.[130]

Clearly, this is a mouthful. Most of us believe in God, and most of us would like to think that this God thinks and cares about us. But not too many of us are willing to accept that this God became like one of us, much less as a person named Jesus. Who wants to believe in a finite and limited God, a God who became a person as frail and weak as we? Furthermore, who wants to think that God became bound by space and time? What kind of a God would this be?

But this is precisely John's point. Unless God became a human being, unless the God who created the universe made himself visible in what he made, we could not know him as he really is. Unless the eternally living one became subject to mortality, bent over, as are we, with the limitations of existential experience, we could not know him as he is.[131] Though he may seem to speak to us, though we may have intimations or thoughts of his reality and presence, unless he appeared to us as a palpable and understandable physical presence we would not know for sure that these experiences had any basis in fact. We would not know for sure that they were really of God, or that God was really there. But now

---

130 Martin Luther, *Commentary on Galatians* (Seattle: CreateSpace, 2010).

131 Or as Athanasius puts it in his *On the Incarnation,* "He [God] became himself an object for the senses" (New York: St. Vladimir's Seminary Press, 1996).

we do. God as Jesus as Word became flesh tells us that God is real, as real as anything else we know or believe to be so. When Word became flesh, definitive explanation of reality became possible: God could be known. The speech of all origins, the communication behind all communication appeared in living and substantive form. And it spoke to us, spoke to us in a way that we could easily understand. It did not speak to us indirectly, that is, through the earth, water, and sky of myth and legend, but directly and personally, communicating itself squarely into our lives, a being like us. We could not miss it. Paradoxically, God became less so that we could become more, could become more knowledgeable about him and, consequently, learn more fully what is most important and meaningful in this often troubling existence. God descended so that we could ascend, so that we could rise out of our spiritual darkness and find true life, what life is most meant to be.[132]

In Jesus, we therefore see and hear the voice of God. In Jesus, we see and hear the eternal speech of the eternal speaker, in Jesus we see and attest to the reality of the eternally existing speech, the endless and sustaining divine providence and communicative pleasure with which God created and upholds the entire universe. In Jesus, God speaks. And he speaks in ways that everyone can understand. No longer is God opaque. The veil has been lifted for all time.[133]

---

132 For a fascinating dialogue on this most paradoxical point of all, see John Milbank and Slavoj Žižek, *The Monstrosity of Christ,* edited by Creston Davis (Cambridge: MIT Press, 2009. In dense yet profound langauge, Žižek ably articulates the difficulties of embracing Jesus as God, yet also affirms that, paradoxically, the nature of the universe dictates that he cannot be understood in any other way.

133 As Augustine put it in his *The Literal Meaning of Genesis,* God directs the disclosure of the "generations that he laid up in creation when it was first established." In Jesus, God sustains all things. See *St. Augustine,*

Put another way, in Jesus, we see the face of God.[134]

These are revolutionary words beyond imagination. Because the uncaused beginning became as one of us, anyone could communicate with it, could communicate with it as does one human being to another. Those who engage in speech could now communicate with the source of speech, the one whose speech set the world into motion, the one whose speech and personality enabled communication to break forth in the cosmos, the one who enabled the universe and all that is in it to speak, function, and express itself in meaningful ways (see Genesis 1:1-31). Now communicating with the ultimate beginning of the universe would become as easy as talking to the person walking or sitting next to you, for now human and God are both flesh and blood human beings. No longer an "it," the uncaused beginning had become a fully gendered person, a person whose name was Jesus, a fully functioning human life. All walls had fallen, all fences had come down. Eternal meaning was here, God embodied and expressed in Word became flesh.[135]

To put it another way, the *kairos* ("time") had come. After many millennia of communicating himself in countless other ways, God appeared visibly on earth, as physically and materially real as you and I are real today.[136] In Jesus, Word became flesh; in Jesus, God made himself physically and definitively known.

Volume I: The Literal Meaning of Genesis in *Ancient Christian Writers*, edited by John Hammond Taylor (New York: Paulist, 1982).

134 Jesus thus fulfills the age old Hebrew longing, denied to Moses (Exodus 33) and expressed most eloquently in the psalms (for instance, Psalm 27:8), to see the face of God (*peniel*), the living face of the divine.

135 In word, as Eberhard Jüngel puts, "God is present." See Jüngel's *God as the Mystery of the World*, translated by Darrell L. Guder (Grand Rapids: William E. Eerdmans, 1983).

136 As Paul puts it in his letter to the church in Galatia, "In the fullness of time, God sent forth his Son, born of a woman, born under the Law

What had long been an expectation, a prophetic expectation enshrined and shaped over many centuries of memory and longing, had now been encapsulated and presented in language, visible and physical language that everyone could see, memory no longer, the future now come.[137]

Or as the church father Ignatius of Antioch observed, in Jesus, God "broke his silence."[138]

Put another way, God spoke.[139]

Let us now return to an issue we have mentioned before. If God became mortal and ceased to be God, would his life still be of any use to us? Clearly, we gain nothing if the creator of the universe appeared to us, lived among us, then died, along with everyone else, as mortal as they. What good would a dead God be? Only if God became flesh while remaining God, only if God became flesh while remaining eternal and infinite would his advent be of any value to us. Only if the source of communication and speech demonstrated that it could communicate itself to us while still functioning as our eternal source of meaning would it offer us any hope for our lives, any hope for finding genuine truth and meaning

---

so that He might redeem those who were under the Law, that we might receive the adoption as sons" (Galatians 4:4-5).

137 For a highly insightful look at the role of memory in language and historical imagination, see Eviatar Zerubavel, *Time Maps* (Chicago: University of Chicago, 2003).

138 See Ignatius' *Letter to the Magnesians* (8:2) in *Ancient Christian Writers,* edited by James A. Kleist (New York: Paulist Press, 1978).

139 If we wish to look at this in a larger picture, we can think about *Kumulipo,* the Hawaiian creation chant, and how it presents the visible "word" or "expression" of the gods as the pinnacle and final goal of the creation. See *The Kumulipo,* translated and edited by Martha Warren Beckwith (Chicago: University of Chicago, 1951, University of Hawaii, 1972).

in our experience. If meaning dies, was it really ultimate meaning?

Happily, this is not what happened. Meaning did not die, nor did meaning disappear. As John puts it in the next part of verse 14, when Word became flesh, "We saw his glory, glory as of the only begotten from the Father." When people saw Word became flesh, that is, Jesus, they saw the glory (Greek *doxa*, Hebrew *kabod*), that expression, be it splendor (for the Jewish audience) or lightning and thunder (for the Greek readers) of God which most people had long identified with God's presence.[140] As far as John's audience, Jew as well as Greek, was concerned, only God could have genuine glory (for the Jew, a glory that surpassed that of all earthly kings; for the Greek, a glory that eclipsed the rudiments of human achievement lauded in the Homeric epics[141]); anything that was genuinely glorious could only be God. When people beheld Word became flesh, they were therefore looking at the glory of God, the spectacular marvel of the divine, the overwhelmingly amazing and seminal expression of what was most real and true come suddenly before them. To see glory in Word became flesh was to see a supernal and full-orbed picture of the creator of the cosmos. Jesus was the glory of God.

In attaching God's glory to Word (Jesus) while also observing that the eternal Word had became flesh, John was saying that even though God became a human being, he remained God. Put another way, Word was human, but Word was, at the same time, always and forever God. It's

---

140 From the Greek word *thambos*, a root of the English word thaumaturgic, meaning miracles or magic: something extraordinary, something outside normal parameters of thought and perception.

141 Specifically, *The Odyssey*, his account of Ulysses's journey and homecoming, and *The Iliad*, his rendering of the events of the Trojan War.

paradoxical, yes, but we have already seen that paradox, properly understood, is the only way that we can reconcile our desire to know meaning and purpose with our fears, reservations, and doubts about how this could possibly happen. As Word became flesh, Jesus communicated the glory of God, patently demonstrating that infinitude could co-exist with the finitude of the realm which it had made. The integrity and essential structure—time, space, and causation—of the universe, as well as the sum totality of the fundamental beingness of God, remained intact. People saw God, and the world did not fall apart. Despite its brush with the finite, eternality continued to be.[142]

And people continued to see in Jesus, God's visible appearance on earth, the fullest possibility of what they could be as human beings. As one writer observed, in Jesus, God reveals "man to himself." He shows humans whom they can be.[143]

In presenting God's glory in fleshly form, Jesus offers us some telling insights into God's character. At the close of verse 14, John states that Word became flesh was "full of grace and truth." What does this mean? We have already defined truth as the most accurate and fullest and ultimate definition of reality, value, and meaning. And we have already established that Word is this truth. When Word

---

142 As the gospel writers observed repeatedly, there is a certain amount of fear involved in coming to find one's true meaning. Time and time again, they write that after Jesus performed a miracle, the people who saw it "feared" (Luke 7:16, to name just one). The visibility of divine power and insight overwhelmed them—as it should for us. For a cinematic take on this, see Franco Zeffirelli's 1977 production, *Jesus of Nazareth*.

143 See the Second Vatican Council's "Pastoral Constitution on the Church in the Modern World" in *Vatican Council II: Constitutions, Decrees, Declarations*, edited by Austin Flannery (Northport, New York: Cotello, 1996).

appeared as flesh, we therefore come to see, definitively, truth in our experience, truth in human form. Although in the past we might have *thought* we had identified truth, might have *thought* that we had uncovered the real meaning of the cosmos, we could not know for certain we had. Even if we tried to connect our perception to the idea of transcendent meaning, we could not know for sure that we had, could not know with certitude that we had in fact found or communicated with genuine realities beyond us. In Jesus, in Word became flesh, however, all this changed. Truth was unmistakably before us.

In verse 17 (refer to the verses quoted above) John enlarges on this idea. In Jesus, the Word became flesh, he insists, truth has "come to be." In Jesus, in Word, truth has appeared, physically and directly, in our lives. The absolute standard, the standard by which all things are evaluated and judged and defined and measured, the standard of value which most accurately explains and frames reality, is before us. That most unyielding of epistemological formulation has now become part of that in which we live every day. The bedrock of all meaning has appeared to us, and truth is here, more real than we can possibly imagine. Ultimate value and understanding stand visible before us. How can we ever be the same?

We cannot. As Moses changed when he witnessed the burning bush in the deserts of Sinai (see Exodus 3), as Paul (then named Saul) changed when Jesus confronted him on the road to Damascus (Acts 9), as the Ethiopian eunuch changed when Philip shared the gospel with him (Acts 8), so will we change when we experience ultimate truth. Our questions receive answers, our longings find fulfillment, our lives fill with value. We know what is genuine, and we know what is real. Our lives become qualitatively different, more different than we can imagine.

But this is the nature of truth. As we noted before, truth is unique. And Word as truth is, too. As a one of a kind, an unmatched singularity, a one-time manifestation of the divine and transcendent God, a sight unlike anything seen before (for never before had God become a human being), Word became flesh is wholly and forever unique, the ultimate encapsulation of truth.[144]

And so it will always be. In Jesus, Word became flesh, truth becomes the most it can be to us.[145]

As we noted earlier, however, we also see in verse 14 the mention of something else: grace. What's grace? In its most basic sense, grace is favor, undeserved favor that one being extends to another. It's love without reward.

We can look at grace in two ways. On the one hand, we humans engage in grace, one to another, every day. We help each other, we look out for each other, we love each other. We are willing to do things for each other that we know we do not necessarily merit or deserve. We enjoy giving freely without thought of return or reward. Why? We believe in each other's fundamental worth as human beings. We believe in ourselves, believe in who we are as fellow travelers on this planet. We believe that people are deserving of love and care, even if those whom we love and care for do nothing for us in return. Whether we know we are doing it or not, we delight in giving grace to one another.

God's grace is similar, though because of who God is, he expresses it in vastly different forms. As the creator and

---

144 We mentioned Exodus 33 earlier, but to describe the story more fully, we can focus on verses 18-23, in which God, after hearing Moses plead with him to let him see him, deigns to show himself, but his backside only. For no one, he tells Moses, can see his face. In Jesus, however, we can.

145 For a good explanation of Jesus' particularity, see John Polkinghorne's *Science and the Trinity: The Christian Encounter with Reality* (New Haven: Yale University, 2004).

sustainer of all that is, God extends grace to us in ways that we finite beings cannot fathom, much less match. One example is the fact of our existence. In his grace, his overwhelming capacity to love, God cared enough about the world and everything in it to bring it and its creatures, including you and me, to life. Our existence is a decisive picture of God's favor toward us.

Another decisive picture of God's grace towards us is the world in which we live. Although it often buckles under the weight of its atrophying forms and structures (think about earthquakes, hurricanes, and tsunamis), the world nevertheless remains a very good world, a very good place to be (see Genesis 1:31). It is beautiful, it is amazing, it is remarkable in its ability to set our hearts aflame with wonder and delight. Thanks to God's grace and the seminal love which impels it, the world is a stunningly marvelous experience.

Still another significant portrait of God's grace toward us is, tellingly enough, Word became flesh. God cared enough about us to give us sentient and meaningful existence, but he also cared enough about us to make himself known to us. By appearing as Word, as Jesus, God chose to reveal himself to us in a way that we could definitively understand him. He, the uncaused beginning and eternal and omnipotent creator, chose to enable us, we most limited of beings, to know him. God's grace is that he cared enough about us to make it possible for us to know *who* made us, to know the source and origin of who we are.

In this grace is embedded perhaps the greatest grace of all. We no longer wonder why we are here, no longer wonder why we are the way we are, no longer wonder why the world is as it is. We know where we began, we know where we are going, and we know where we will end. We have answers to our deepest questions, solutions to our most profound riddles. Existential understanding is within our grasp.

God's grace is that we can begin to understand the meaning of existence.[146]

At its core, grace expresses the innermost character of God: love. God loves us, God cares about us, God desires to shower us with compassion and favor every day of our lives. Graciousness is intrinsic and integral to whom he is.[147]

Hence, when we read that Word was full of grace and truth, or that grace and truth came to be in Jesus (verse 17), not only do we understand that ultimate value is now visible and accessible in our experience, we also acknowledge that in Word we see a visible picture of the innermost character of God. In Word became flesh we see that God is love, that although God is righteous, powerful, and holy, he is also about love, a singularly powerful and compelling love. And in Jesus we see the most tangible and poignant picture of this love, God's great and longsuffering love for humanity and the world he made. In Jesus we see the love which God most wants for us to experience in this life.[148]

As the apostle Paul writes in his letter to his protégé Titus, Jesus is the "kindness of God" (Titus 3:4). In Jesus,

---

146 Another dimension of God's grace is the idea of his providence, his comprehensive care for us and the creation. This is depicted beautifully in Carlos Eire's *Learning to Die in Miami* (New York: Free Press, 2010).

147 A full description of the grace of God could occupy many, many pages. One recent and practical meditation on grace is Philip Yancey's *What's So Amazing About Grace?* (Grand Rapids: Zondervan, 1997). Also, although we humans will always wrestle with God's goodness in the face of evil, we can also understand that, in some often incomprehensible ways, God's grace addresses even these very difficult questions. But this is a discussion outside the scope of this book.

148 For more thoughts, put simply but profoundly, on God's love for us, read the epistle 1 John, which the apostle wrote some years after he penned the gospel we are studying.

God visibly expresses his care and compassion for human beings.

To sum up, for John to say that Word became flesh was "full of grace and truth," or as he puts it in verse 17, "grace and truth came to be" in Jesus, is for him to say that a surpassing love and favor, a love and favor that overwhelms all others, and truth, the absolute and unassailable value that governs and explains all of reality are now part of and fully visible and available in the human experience. Although given our finitude, we will still not be able, even in the face of Word became flesh, to see and know *everything* about our lives and the life of the world, we can at least begin to grasp and connect with one who does. In Word become flesh life therefore finds its ultimate destiny. Not only does Word provide a picture of the gestational speech of the universe, it furnishes a portrait of its inner being, its soul as well. In Jesus, we see the heart of God.

Word as God became flesh means that we have a God who not only created and gave truth and meaning to the entire universe but a God who entered this universe and expressed this truth and meaning, physically and directly, to those in it. Word as God became flesh means that we can now understand the universe, and we can now understand God. All that we ever imagined about wonder and significance in this life we can now begin to cultivate and grasp. God has come, and he has come in a way that we can understand. We can see God as one of us, fully mortal and human, yet we can continue to see him as God, wholly infinite and eternal.

Before we go on, let us note one more point in verse 14. John emphasizes that people "saw" (or, as some translations would have it, "beheld") Word became flesh. The verb that John uses here to describe the act of seeing has its roots in a work by Plato called *Theaetetus.* In *Theaetetus,* Plato argues that knowledge is more than mere perception. Real knowledge, he argues, is to see beyond what is visible, to see between the lines, as it were, and know that there is more to the world than what meets the immediate eye. John therefore wants to say that when people "saw" Word became flesh in Jesus, they were doing more than seeing. They were *understanding*. They were understanding that Word was more than a mere human being, that there was more to Word than what they could see in its flesh and blood physicality.[149]

To see Jesus as Word became flesh was therefore to engage in no ordinary act of seeing. It was rather to see something more extraordinary than anyone could have imagined. It was to see God. When John writes that people "saw" Word became flesh he was conveying their experience of an event unique in all of human history: the visible and materially comprehensible appearance of God.[150]

The last part of verse 18 (the final verse in what the Christian church calls John's "prologue") amplifies this point. It states that Word *explains* God. John's use of this word is particularly acute. It is a word, εξηγεομαι, which only appears only a few times in the New Testament text. Εξηγεομαι, was a technical term, rarely used in everyday conversation, which some Greek poets used to explicate or announce, among other things, information about life or, more importantly, revelation about the gods. By using εξηγεομαι to describe the effects of Word, John is reinforcing what he has been saying all along. Word, in the person of Jesus, is an announcement, a proclamation and revelation about God. Word reveals God.

---

149 See the *Theaetetus of Plato* as we mentioned it above.

150 It is also worth saying that although John's Greek audience knew of numerous attestations in their mythology of the gods appearing on earth (the story of Zeus and Io is one example), his Jewish readers had long believed, as John puts it at one point in verse 18, "no one [even the much revered Moses (see the story from Exodus we cited above)] has seen God at any time."

In Word, in Jesus, we see a singularly profound disclosure of the infinite and eternal God.

Put another way, Jesus is the doorway to God. When we open the door to Jesus, we open a door to God.[151]

If we bring all this together, our conclusions about Word as God, divine glory, and grace and truth, we can say that, broadly speaking, Word became flesh makes God knowable, makes him understandable, more knowable and understandable than he has ever been before. Word became flesh is the unique explanation and definitive revelation of God in our earthly lives. It is the singular presentation of God in the human experience, a one and only time expression of the personal metaphysical to us. Because of Word became flesh, we can know God, can know and understand him as a fellow traveler in our life experience. Although God will always remain in many ways an impenetrable somethingness, a mysterious presence hovering in and over reality, in Word became flesh he has become as personal and knowable and explainable as our finite minds can possibly conceive him to be. In Jesus, the eternal Word became mortal flesh, we can become friends with God.

And a friendly and explained God means a friendly and explained world. No longer do we need to see the world as a place of loneliness, emptiness, and alienation. No longer do we need to see the world as a place where people are born and die seemingly without cause or point, a place where good as well as bad things seem to happen for no rhyme or reason. Despite all that happens in it, we can see living in the world as an inherently meaningful experience.

As a result, although we will always wonder why life

---

151 See also John 10:7, in which Jesus calls himself the door to the sheep, the sheep being those who hear and respond positively to the voice of God.

happens as it does, and yes, we will always wonder why we are the way we are, Word became flesh reminds us that, even if we do not see them, answers are there. Ultimately, not one question will remain. Life will not always be an unsolvable puzzle, an aching abyss and bottomless pit of epistemological darkness and existential uncertainty. We can begin to unmask an answer to the greatest mystery of all: why?

Communication is at hand, too. As we all know, when people talk with each other, they learn about each other. They get to know each other's likes and dislikes, each other's hopes and dreams, each other's dreads and fears, each other's happiness and joys. Further, if the timing and chemistry are right, they become friends, people who enjoy each other, who rely on each other, who look out for each other. In time, again, if the chemistry is particularly good, they become best friends, dedicated to always look out for the best interests of the other. They are inseparable.[152]

So it is with us and Word and, by extension, God. We become God's friend, and God becomes ours. We get to know God, and God gets to know us. We develop an intimate relationship with the one who made us. We learn about meaning from the one who made meaning, dig into truth with the one who creates and ensures its presence in the universe. We learn deeply about the most important things, learn about them from the one who created and made them important. We learn about and get to know the speech, the living and personal speech that created the world.

In short, God speaks to us, and we speak back. We experience steady communion with our creator. In Word became flesh, we see everything we need to see.

---

152 Moreover, as Dean Radin points out in his *Entangled Minds* (New York: Simon and Schuster, 2006), the essential nature of the universe is entanglement, and those of like mind and heart inevitably tend to "gravitate" toward one another.

One issue, however, remains. It has to do with uniqueness and singularity. Although we have discussed this in regard to Word and truth, we need to address one more dimension of it. Outside the testimony of the New Testament, how do we know that Word became flesh is the only way in which God appeared as one of us?

Let's first recall that John identifies Word became flesh as "the only begotten from the Father" (see verse 14 above). As there is only one God (if there were more than one God, we wouldn't have a "real" God, for none of them would be worth having as "God"), there is only one Word became flesh. God chose only one way to manifest and display himself, only one way to disclose who he really is to the world.

He could not have done otherwise. If God is the only God, then it follows that this only God would only appear in one way. If there were multiple gods, then, yes, these multiple gods would appear in many different ways. But there is only one God, so he will appear in only one way.

But wait, you may be asking: cannot this God appear in different ways to fit the situations of different people? He probably could. What we need to focus on, however, is not so much how God appears to us but how we *experience* him. Everyone is different and everyone will experience things, including God, in different ways. This doesn't mean, however, that God must be a different God, qualitatively and physically speaking, to different people; this would splinter God beyond repair. It rather means that although God does not change and although God is not a multiplicity of beings, we humans change constantly. We have nearly infinite possibilities of being.

For this reason, it is not God who must change to accommodate us, but we who must change (or, properly speaking, *be* changed) to know and experience him. Though our experience of God will vary greatly, God remains the same. He must. Otherwise, he would not be an eternal God. Word became flesh is the only expression of God that has appeared to humanity, yes, but how we *experience* Word became flesh is a function of what each of us billions of humans is. We all are unique.

And so is God. He must be. Otherwise, he would not be worth thinking about as God. He would be a God whom we make ourselves, hardly a worthy deity. And as God is unique, so will his physical appearance be.

How do we know that Word is the only *physical* manifestation of God? How do we know that Jesus is the only mortal image of God? We know because we know that Word reflects, in every way, who God is, and if, as we observed, God is unique, Word must be, too. As the law of non-contradiction demands that red cannot be blue, so it requires that God cannot be two "Words" at once. Either God is *the* Word, or he is not. Similarly, either Jesus is God, or he is not. Furthermore, as we shall see, as God in the flesh, Jesus had a unique mission to fulfill on earth, a mission which only one Word (and one Jesus) could fulfill. As there can only be one Word, so can there be only one Jesus. And there can only be one Jesus because only one Jesus could accomplish the task Jesus was sent to do.[153]

So what do we have? We have a personal and infinite creator Word who as God is the center and beginning of reality, meaning, and truth, and who at a particular point in space and time history disclosed himself in the form of a person named Jesus. And in Jesus we therefore see the presentation, in human form, of the fullness of meaning, reality, and truth, the essential expression of the infinite and personal creator God. In Jesus we see the manifestation of God and all that he is in visible substance, shape, and form. Because he is God

---

153 Again, refer to John Polkinghorne's book we cited above.

and human simultaneously, Jesus ensures that God, as Word, communicates himself in material reality while remaining the infinite and eternal God. In Jesus, time, space, eternity, and meaning coalesce in cosmic unity, announcing the fact and presence of God in a way that makes him and his truth potentially available to everyone who has ever lived on planet Earth. In Jesus, we see the fullness of God.[154]

In addition, we can say that, the existentialists and their quite accurate conclusions (if there is no God) about existence notwithstanding, we do not need to succumb to the observations of the ancient philosopher Lucretius who, writing in the first century B.C., said, "Divinity exists in remote inaccessible recesses of which we know nothing; but with us it has no dealing, with us it has no relation." To the contrary: because Word—God—became flesh in a genuinely historical person named Jesus, we can know God. No longer is God remote, but fully accessible and deliberately oriented toward us.

As a result, we can commune with God, safely and freely, now and forevermore.[155]

Let us bring some things together. Our original thesis was the centrality of speech, in any number of forms and expressions, human as well as divine, in existence. Speech is the starting point of reality and meaning, that which

---

154 Clearly, as we have already noted, to say that Jesus is God and human simultaneously is not easy. It is a conclusion bound up in an ultimately impenetrable mystery. Theologians call this union of human and divine the "theandric" union, an unmixed juxtaposition of divinity and mortality in one person. Without veering into theological solipsism about this, however, we are best to accept it as yet another necessary paradox undergirding our human quest for and engagement in the fullness of the divine.

155 On this, see Lucretius' De rerum natura (On the Nature of Things), translated by Ronald Latham (New York: Penguin, 1951).

necessarily ensures that we and the life we live have value and purpose. Speech is the foundation of truth in the universe, and speech is the foundation of personal experience in a personal world. Without speech, neither we nor the world would be, and without speech, neither we nor the world would have any meaning. A speechless (in the broadest possible sense) existence contradicts itself. Speech ensures movement, space and time motion, revelation, and exchange in the cosmos. Speech embodies life, and speech is essential to a purposeful existential experience. Speech expresses the fundamental meaningfulness of the creation.

So where does speech come from? Early on, we observed that speech could not come from impersonal substance, could not come from something that has no communicative capacity or awareness. To say that nothingness can express itself is to violate the nature of nothingness. What was never there can ever possibly be. Communication cannot arise in a vacuum. Speech must come from personal beingness.

And where does this personal beingness come from?

It has to come from a "someone," a "someone" with intelligence, form, value, presence, and purpose. It has to come from someone who *wants* to communicate and establish communication, someone who wants to establish and ensure the factuality and presence of speech in the universe.

And this someone, it follows, must be a someone who is, in some unfathomable way, before all other "someones." It has to be a someone who has the power to originate and create, who has the ability to bring the nonexistent into existence, someone with exceeding and sovereign creativity and imagination. This someone must be someone who existed before anything else began.

Who is this someone? In John's gospel, we have the answer: Word. In Word, the αρχη, the necessarily personal absolute and eternal and uncaused beginning, we see this someone, this someone who is the infinite and personal creator of all things. And we also see a name: Jesus. In Jesus as Word is, disclosed for all time, the ultimate speech, the eternal point from which all other speech began, the profoundly personal genesis of all that is.

In addition to acknowledging the centrality of speech in life and existence, we observed that the world speaks, that the world is a place of speech, communication, and revelation. The world is a fount of disclosure. And the world is meaningful. The world is meaningful because it was created, intentionally spoken into existence by a meaningful and personal Word who endowed it and the beings living in it with personality, speech, and communicative capacities. A created world is a meaningful world, and a created world is a revelatory world. It speaks.

John's gospel further tells us that because we live in a meaningful world, we live in a world that can be explained. It can be understood. Indeed, as we saw, if the world has no meaning, we will never, as the existentialists so cogently grasped, understand it. We will never know what it really is. Moreover, we will never really know who we are. We will remain, to use Sartre's words once more, "useless passions."

And how can we understand and explain this meaningful world? We explain it with Word. And how do we explain it with Word? We explain it in the event to which we have devoted many pages of this meditation: Word became flesh. In Word became flesh we find existential explanation in fullest form, God's most complete presentation (to date) of his person and ways.[156] In Word became flesh we see speech embodied and verified and presented as the ground of all meaning and

---

156 Or as the apostle Paul puts it in his first letter to the church at Corinth, Jesus is the "wisdom of God" (1 Corinthians 1:24, 30), the fullest picture of God's intentions for time, eternity, and the human race. And we say "to date" because according to the New Testament, on one day to come Jesus

purpose. In Word became flesh, expressed and centered in the person of Jesus, we see disclosed the essence of the ultimate speech and truth without which neither we nor the cosmos could function. Word became flesh is the meaning for which we have been looking all our lives, the meaning that answers all our prayers and longings. In Word became flesh, in God becoming human in the person of Jesus Christ, is embodied the foundational speech, the guiding apex of language and communication upon which all else is built. Jesus as Word became flesh brings explanation home.[157]

It all comes down to speech. What we said at the very beginning about speaking still holds true. When we speak, we really do bring something to life, really do bring it, in a palpable and engaging way, into our experience. We usher it into our purview, invite it into what we know and believe, birth it in how we live. We give it reality, perceptible and knowable reality. Speech constructs our world.

So why do we speak? We speak because we are communicative beings who live in a communicative universe. And why are we communicative beings who live in a communicative universe? We are communicative beings who live in a communicative universe because we and the universe are the uniquely personal creations of a communicative, eternal, and personal Word. In its fundamental and creative eternality, the forever and everlasting communicative Word spoke, spoke the entire universe into being. Speech created the universe. And speech created you and me. We are the products of speech, the personal products of a personal and communicative being who, through his speech, his living

---

will return to display and present himself in even more startling form to humanity (see Revelation 19).

157   As Jesus puts in the eighth and ninth chapters of John's gospel, "I am the light of the world" (John 8:12, 9:5).

word that illuminates his actions, brought us and the universe to life. We are personal beings who have been directly and intentionally communicated into existence.

And we have purpose. We know that someone wants us to be here. And because we know that someone wants us to be here, we can also know that we are not alone. Someone is looking out for us, someone is gazing upon us. Someone cares about us. We are loved.

And we are loved with a love that is eternal, a love that extends beyond this existence, a love that will never end. Even as we leave this existence (which we all will one day do), we will not leave unnoticed, will not leave forgotten and alone. We will continue to experience God's love for us, the grace and truth that "came to be" in Word became flesh, in Jesus Christ. We will know God's love forever and eternally. God is a living God, an eternally living God whose mind and heart (in an anthropomorphic sense) are permanently set in eternity, and his love is no different. It is forever.[158]

There is a catch to all this, however. It is this: if we are to continue reading John's account of Jesus' life, we will see that Jesus did not come merely to present God to the world. He came so that we might know God. He came to provide a means for us to know and experience God. Yes, in Jesus, meaning has come, but every one of us must decide to believe and accept this meaning for it to become *real* for us. Every one of us must make a decision to believe that in Jesus, meaning, ultimate meaning has indeed come into our experience. Every one of us must decide to believe that Jesus, as John records Jesus saying on the eve of his death, is "the way, the truth, and the life" (John 14:6), the only way to God and the

---

158 As one song puts it, "He knows my name, He knows my every thought, He knows each tear that falls, and He hears me when I call." ("He Knows My Name" by Tommy Walker, copyright 1996, Doulos Publishing.)

eternal meaning and embrace he offers to every human being. Every one of us must chose to take hold of this wonderful gift that Jesus as Word became flesh brings to the world. Not only must we *listen* to God, but we must *believe* in God, believe that he really is there, believe that he really does care, believe that he really did come to earth as Jesus Christ.[159]

And what is the precise content of this most wonderful of gifts? It is the gift of salvation, the gift of forgiveness and eternal life. In salvation, God, the holy and righteous creator, forgives and forgets our transgressions and sins, expiates our guilt, and reconciles us to him. God makes us part of his eternal family, a fellow heir of his forever kingdom. Salvation is God's way of making us whole and complete, fully able to commune with and enjoy him, now and eternally. Salvation brings God to us in the most meaningful way possible. It allows us to throw off the grip of sin, the sin that blinds us, the sin that keeps us apart from God, the sin that prevents us from experiencing everything that God has for us. Salvation enables us to pursue our true destiny, to know the fullness of God. Salvation sets us free.[160]

And how do we obtain this gift of salvation, this forgiveness of our sins and entrance into the eternal life of God? We obtain it by believing that when Jesus died on the

---

159 On this, see John 8:43, where John records Jesus telling the Jewish leaders of his day that although they hear him, they do not *really* hear. Sadly, they miss the whole point of who Jesus was. To look at this from another angle, consider that the Hebrew word for hearing (*shama*) describes a hearing that *obeys*, a hearing that truly understands what it hears, and responds in kind.

160 Indeed, as the historian R. G. Collingwood pointed out, we cannot separate the metaphysical from morality. If Jesus is God, the ultimate expression of metaphysical purpose, then this purpose is inexorably moral. Salvation is therefore intrinsic to the human experience. See Fred Ingles's profile of Collingwood in his *History Man* (Princeton, New Jersey: Princeton University, 2011).

cross, a cross on which he was placed, unjustly, by the Roman authorities of his day, he died for us, died for us so that we could receive God's forgiveness of our sins and step into eternal life with him. God's forgiveness is grounded in the ultimate paradox of Word became flesh. What has always lived, the personal and eternal God, died a mortal's death, died as he never ought to do, to ensure that the humans he created would not die as *they* ought to do, so that they could live as they had originally been destined to do. Jesus died so that we would never again experience the angst and heartbreak of this mortal existence. He died so that we could spend eternity with God. What had always been ceased to exist so that what was destined to end would never do so again. Jesus died so that we might live forever, so that we might enjoy endless existence and communion with God, the personal and conscious and uncaused God who birthed the world, the eternal God whose gracious speech of truth brought all things to life. As the great fourteenth century mystic Julian of Norwich remarked, Jesus died so that we could experience God's "bliss," the "bliss" of knowing him as the "fullness of joy" and the light of "endless day."[161]

How did Jesus do this? After Jesus died to propitiate (satisfied the penalty of God's wrath for) our sins, he rose again. He was resurrected, alive forevermore. God is a living God. God is an eternal God, a God who always lives, and a God who resurrects *all* who believe in him. Guaranteed. Even if those who find meaning in Jesus as Word became flesh die (as we all will), they will live again. As John records Jesus telling a follower named Martha shortly before he was

---

161 Julian of Norwich, *Showings*, chapters 46 and 83, translated by Edmund Colledge (New York: Paulist Press, 1978). See also famous evangelist Billy Graham's thoughts on living eternally with God in his *Nearing Home: Life, Faith, and Finishing Well* (Nashville: Thomas Nelson, 2011).

crucified, "I am the resurrection and the life; he who believes in Me will live even if he dies, and everyone who lives and believes in me will never die" (John 11:25-26).

So it was that Jesus told John when he appeared to him in a vision on the island of Patmos (where John had been exiled by the Roman authorities late in the first century A.D.), "I am the first and the last, and the living One; and I became dead, and behold, I am alive forevermore" (Revelation 1:17-18). Jesus, the eternal Word, indeed died, yet he lives eternally. Paradoxical? Perhaps. But it is the paradox that fully explains the final and ultimate meaning of existence.[162]

So we do not run away. We do not conclude that we are useless passions without meaning in a meaningless world, do not conclude that we are dust and dirt, and nothing more. We instead conclude that because we have been created with speech, the meaningful speech of a meaningful creator who freely chose to speak us and the cosmos into being, we have more meaning than we can possibly imagine. We conclude that although we will never understand everything about our existence, we can understand and communicate with one who does. We conclude that if we choose to embrace the full truth of Word became flesh, that Jesus is indeed God become human being, the eternal fount of truth and meaning made visible in material experience, we will see and grasp everything we need to know. And we understand that one day, life will no longer be a frustratingly finite and heartbreakingly terminal mystery. We will know.[163]

---

162 Peter understood this very well when, in the sixth chapter of John's gospel, he replied to Jesus' queries about whether he and the apostles, too, would leave him that, "To whom shall we go, Lord? You have words of eternal life (John 6:68).

163 On this, see Paul's words in 1 Corinthians 13:12 (part of which we looked at earlier): "For now we see in a mirror dimly, but then face to face; now I [we] know in part, but then I [we] will know fully just as I [we] also

Yet it all begins, as does everything else: with speech. So, speak. Speak and experience who you are, speak and experience who you can be, speak and experience the truth about the way the world is made. Most importantly, speak, and know and believe that God is there, listening and ready to respond. Speak and experience your creator, speak and know your maker. Speak and find the meaning that is your true life and home.

Speak.

---

have been fully known. Or consider John's observations in his first epistle: "Beloved, now we are children of God, and it has not appeared as yet what we will be. We know that when He appears, we will be like Him, because we will see Him just as He is" (1 John 3:2). One day, we will definitively know—everything.

About the Author

A writer and teacher, William E. Marsh holds graduate degrees in theology, philosophy, and history. *It's All in a Word* is his fourth book.